# BYWORD

# BYWORD

A Nation Called Out Of Their Name

Elder Mark Makabi

Copyright © 2016 All Rights Reserved
Print ISBN: 978-0-692-03191-9
E-book ISBN: 978-0-692-03199-5
LCCN: 2016940217

Black Cumin Cseedz Publishing, an imprint of
Bitter Herbsz Enterprise, LLC
P.O. Box 327
Smyrna, GA 30081-0327

Edited by: Michael ben Michael
Researcher: Elder Makabi
Additional Research Contribution: Michael ben Michael
Cover Designed by: Ernestine's Echo imprint of BHE, LLC
All poetic and spoken word expressions created & written by:
Elder Makabi and Mark-Alan

All Bible quotations are taken from
the King James & the New International versions.

*This book may not be reproduced, transmitted, or stored in whole or in part by any means, including graphic, electronic, or mechanical formats without the expressed written consent of the publisher except in the case of brief quotations embodied in critical, professionally-reviewed articles and reviews.*

Amazon: www.amazon.com/author/markmakabi
Facebook: www.facebook.com/eldermarkmakabi
Twitter: www.twitter.com/bywordthebook
YouTube: www.youtube.com/c/eldermarkmakabi

*The views and opinions of the authors expressed herein does not necessarily reflect the positions and/or views of the whole Biblical nation of Israel; moreover, the author is currently not affiliated or associated with any civil rights, religious, Hebrew-Israelite, human rights, activist, or political groups or organizations that may share, express, and/or claim to be Hebrews, Israelites, and/or Jews and all of their views and opinions do not necessarily reflects the authors'*

*The official national identity reference book for the descendants of the Transatlantic slave trade in the Americas.*

COMING SOON!
MARK MAKABI
NEXT BOOK
**"BIBLEPHOBIA"**
*Bible-phobia*

# Contents

| | |
|---|---|
| Introduction | 5 |
| Chapter One | |
| From Jerusalem to Jamestown | 15 |
| Chapter Two | |
| The Shame of Slavery | 45 |
| Chapter Three | |
| Baptized into the Religion of Slavery! | 66 |
| Chapter Four | |
| Slave Codes for Black Codes | 91 |
| Chapter Five | |
| Byword | 119 |
| Chapter Six | |
| The Byword Was Made Flesh! | 149 |
| Chapter Seven | |
| The Power of the Negro Spirituals! | 190 |
| CNN News: Who is Black in America? | 231 |

BYWORD REFERENCES GUIDE FOR A NATION CALLED OUT OF THEIR NAME

| | |
|---|---|
| Cimmarrones | 22 |
| Afro-Nicaraguans | 23 |
| Africans | 25 |
| Afro-Latinos | 28 |
| Moors | 30 |
| Afro-Antilleans | 32 |
| Black British | 34 |
| Dominicans | 36 |
| Kittitians | 39 |
| Tobagonians | 40 |
| Puerto Ricans | 50 |
| Cape Verdeans | 51 |
| Americo-Liberians | 53 |
| Black-Caribs | 54 |
| Guadeloupeans | 54 |
| Afro-Belizeans | 57 |
| Afro-Arubans | 58 |
| Bermudians | 60 |
| Dominica | 61 |
| Nevisians | 63 |
| Blacks | 73 |
| Afro-Brazilians | 75 |
| Mulattos | 77 |
| Afro-Black Canadians | 78 |
| Afro-Peruvians | 80 |
| Panamanians | 81 |
| Afro-French Guianese | 83 |
| Martinicans | 84 |
| Afro-Paraguayans | 86 |
| Caymanians | 87 |
| Afro-Cubans | 101 |

| | |
|---|---|
| Jamaicans | 103 |
| Creoles | 104 |
| Afro-Mexicans | 106 |
| Colored People | 107 |
| Montserratians | 109 |
| Afro-Curacaoans | 110 |
| Afro-Venezuelans | 112 |
| Maroons | 114 |
| Afro-Hondurans | 115 |
| U.S. Virgin Islanders | 126 |
| Barbadians | 127 |
| Afro-Costa Ricans | 129 |
| Afro-Uruguayans | 131 |
| Vincentians | 132 |
| African-Americans | 133 |
| Guyanese | 139 |
| Trinidadians | 140 |
| Quilomobos | 142 |
| Gullah/Geechee | 143 |
| Barbudans | 175 |
| Anguillans | 176 |
| Afro-Chileans | 177 |
| St. Lucians | 178 |
| Bahamians | 179 |
| Afro-Bolivians | 181 |
| Grenadians | 182 |
| Afro-Surinamese | 183 |
| Afro-Colombians | 185 |
| Negroes | 187 |
| Bonairians | 200 |
| West Indies | 201 |
| Hispanics | 202 |

| | |
|---|---:|
| British Virgin Islanders | 204 |
| Nigger | 205 |
| Afro-Argentines | 207 |
| Afromestizo-Salvadorans | 209 |
| Guatemalans-Garifuna | 210 |
| Saban | 211 |
| Afro-Ecuadorians | 213 |
| Turks & Caicos Islanders | 216 |
| Haitians | 217 |
| Black Seminoles | 218 |
| Antiguans | 220 |
| Afro-Caribbeans | 221 |
| The Biblical Nation of Israel | 223 |
| The Invention of White People! | 225 |
| Christians | 228 |

## The Poetic Spoken Words of Elder Makabi & Mark-Alan

| | |
|---|---:|
| *Oscar's Trowel* | 13 |
| *My Walk, My Shoes* | 42 |
| *12 Healing Leaves!* | 64 |
| *Bitter Herbs* | 89 |
| *One Drop Rules!* | 117 |
| *BYWORD UP!* | 144 |
| *Floetic Soul* | 154 |
| *Blurring The Blur Lines* | 188 |
| *Saint Ernestine, My Birthday Blessing* | 215 |
| *eRace* | 239 |

# INTRODUCTION

**Deuteronomy 28:37 (KJV)**
*"And thou shalt become an astonishment, a proverb, and a **BYWORD**, among all nations whither the LORD shall lead thee."*

*Byword* is a product of my self-discovery, human, and righteous development beginning from birth to the present. *Byword* is a revelation in how a people torn from their land are great in number and power, yet miseducation has blinded them to their own truths. *Byword* extends to family, friends, co-workers, education, experiences, events, highlights, and influences, I am compelled to honor my father and mother *(Israelite ancestral heritage)* and their extraordinary resilience's, faith, sacrifices, power, love, endurance, and wisdom they have demonstrated through the ***Israelite (Biblical) holocaust of slavery and all of its forms and experiences in the Americas.*** Therefore, I dedicated *Byword* to my father **Oscar L. McNeil, (91)** who is the head cornerstone of our family, my role model, and in memory of my mother, **Saint Ernestine McNeil (84),** my first educator and teacher in righteousness who recently pass into her eternal rest from all her righteous works, as a testimony and remembrance of their love, patience's, and spiritual (Biblical) guidance.

In the remembrances of the love and support, I recognize my family for their collective influences on my life. My family includes: Grandparents *Thomas and Daisy McNeil, Louis Gray and Viola Moultrie, my siblings Angie, Arnie, Audrey, Annette, Anthony, Alicia, Adonna, Avery, April, Bishop Nathaniel Williams, Mother Viola Ice, Brother Fred McFadden, Aunt Vivian Vandross, Uncle Thomas McNeil, Cousin Ransom McNeil, and all my uncles, aunts, nephews, nieces and cousins.* Thus, I am a living testimony of the Israelite proverb, "Start children off on the way they should go, and even when they are old they will not turn from it. **(Proverbs 22:6)** in correlation to **"it takes a village to raise a child."** My Brockton, Massachusetts roots and my human development at the Full Gospel Tabernacle extends to South Carolina, Maryland, Georgia, and Toronto Canada; this led to the development of *Byword* which I began writing in Georgia and completed in my hometown, Brockton Massachusetts.

*Byword* redefines the true history of the so-called Negro as the true descendants of Israelites in the Americas. ***Byword* leads in the reclassification of the racial and national identity of the slaves from a historical, social, Biblical, psychological, and cultural perspective.** Furthermore, education is the process in which a nation develops their own understanding of themselves, acquiring the fundamental qualities to be effective by accepting personal responsibility from the power of knowledge of self to work in their self-interest. This is established in **Hosea 4:6,** "My people are destroyed for lack of knowledge…" Lack of knowledge allows for enemies to be opportunistic and predatory upon a people who do not know or fully understand themselves. When people are ignorant of themselves, they no longer have a concept of a culture or conglomerate nation of peoples that arise from a common ancestral home. The Israelites in the Americas were enslaved through exploitation of infighting and points at which the anti-Semitism of Europe made it easy to justify enslavement of a great people who were undermined solely based on their envious spirit and foreign lies among them and denial of their greatness.

Knowledge of self is so powerful that if you do not possess it you will be destroyed *racially, psychologically, culturally, socially, economically, sexually, politically, artistically and spiritually.* **"My people" refers to the Israelites who are the *descendant of slaves in the Americas.*** However, *Byword* is an educational contribution for the healing of nations. Nonetheless, racism in America is not going away; therefore, for effective solutions, healing, and progress, the descendants of slaves needs to drink the bitter herbs by taking ownership of their holocaust of slavery.

By honoring and preserving the dignity, legacy, and sacrifices for freedom the Israelites in the Americas made for them. For example, although I support freedom of speech when we embrace, promote, support, and glorify the epithet "nigger" as the derivative, colloquial *term of endearment*, "nigga", we are confirming that we are in fact pieces of property, if not physically psychologically, and we are property as modern slaves in America; in other words, nigger has always been a term of objectifying individuals and reducing them to objects, non-persons. We, the Israelites of the Americas become outraged when the American Caucasians, sons of Japheth, call us niggers. This is hypocritical. We should be outraged when we address each other as niggers. This process begins with humility, being honest with ourselves. You cannot learn about yourself if you do not respect yourself.

However, it is the author's intention via the educational, social, cultural, and spiritual (Biblical) process to make racism within the Americas and their corrupt pejorative, "nigger" non-effective and obsolete. **We need to restore our Israelite family values, development of self-love, education, unity, honor our Israelite (Biblical) holocaust with a slavery memorial, perpetuate righteous aspirations (*e.g. the Ten Commandments*), and formerly separate from the immoral and ethnocentric cultural values of the European Gentile sons of Japheth.** It is the sons of Japheth who have prized acts or ideologies such as abortion, homosexuality, feminism, observing pagan holidays, and eating unclean foods such as pork, seafood, and other scavengers and vermin. Our separation as our Israelite's fathers did coming out of their Babylonian captivity. **Ezra 6:21,** "So the Israelites who had returned from the exile ate it, together with all **who had separated themselves from the unclean practices of their Gentile neighbors** in order to seek the LORD, the God of Israel."

Moreover, our separation from the European sons of Japheth and the nations does not necessarily exclude us from developing respectful, working, social, and/or friendship-based relations with the sons of Japheth or any other nation; however, our separation does include separating our Biblical Israelites values from them spiritually, culturally, morally, psychologically, artistically, politically, and religiously. For example, the author supports the freedom of choice of the European sons of Japheth in the Americas to have abortions and to be homosexuals, leading to the self-extermination of their race; however, these abominable practices are in violation of our Biblical Israelites laws and family values. **Deuteronomy 23:17 "There shall be no whore of the daughters of Israel, nor a sodomite of the sons of Israel."**

We continue to witness America repeating history that leads to self-destruction; these actions surpass even the iniquities of Sodom and Gomorrah. Woe unto America! However, *we should learn the lesson of history from our Israelite (Biblical) holocaust of slavery* in the Americas which should be a mandatory educational requirement as far as the curriculum in all of the public schools in addition to requirements for immigrants seeking citizenship in the Americas. *"The Israelite holocaust of slavery "Honor Thy Father and Mother Memorial Month of Remembrance"* should be a national month of remembrance in the Americas. This month of remembrance should take place in the month of August. It is a month that will honor the contributions and sacrifices for freedom our Israelite ancestors made for us in the Americas and abroad. Our honor, should include the children born of so-called Negro slaves using their God-given resources and talent to produce more informative movies, documentaries, music, plays, books, music videos, artwork, art shows, manufactured goods, schools, and museums concerning their *Israelite (Biblical) holocaust of slavery in the Americas.*

Our vision is to establish a national and international "Israelite (Biblical) Holocaust of Slavery Memorial Month". This "Memorial" month will be a time of remembrance exclusively for and in the best interest of the descendant of slaves. We will own, control, and insure

# BYWORD

the interests and needs of the Israelites in the Americas. None of the following shall undermine the interests and needs of the Israelites of the Americas: no civil rights, equal rights, social movements, human rights activists, political issue, Black lives matter movement, diversity matters, multicultural situations, matters of political correctness, special interest groups, liberals, and conservatives. None of these entities or individuals will undermine, contaminate, compare, integrate, trivialize, used, and/or blur the lines of our 400 years holocaust with their agenda from this point on. These entities will not do anything that is contrary to our Israelite Biblical values as we free ourselves with wisdom. However, these entities are welcome to contribute to the healing of the children of Israel on our terms.

*Byword* is a course for schools, colleges, universities, churches, workshops, seminars, homeschools, and various organizations that contributes to history, humanities, Biblical studies, race relations, social science, and culturally relevant program which I believe will change the face of race in the Americas forever. Furthermore, we need to clarify the blur lines between color and race by correcting the horrific effects from the reclassification of the national and racial identity that was imposed on us by the European Gentile sons of Japheth during colonialism. Moreover, the author respects and understands the sovereignty of nations to classify their national and racial identity in accordance with their cultural concepts of race however the author does not accept any national and racial concepts that is contrary to the truth. Furthermore, the author apologizes in advance for any names, groups, and/or locations that relates to the trans-Atlantic slave trade that is relevant but not mention in the book with the understanding that this book does not proclaims to be conclusive as additional research will produce more information.

*Byword* is a reminder for us to learn that those of us who failed to learn from the evil lessons of history will probably be doomed to repeat it. **These are those among us who choose to be ignorant and blind to the truth.** Therefore, it is imperative that we should study, remember, embrace, and educate ourselves and children about the shame, pain, glory, power, and majesty of our Israelite (Biblical) holocaust of slavery in the Americas. This testimony of our superior character, resilience, and ability to insure it will never happen again. It is time for us as a people to move towards the **CIVIL RIGHTS EXODUS**. The **CIVIL RIGHTS EXODUS** states that…

- We aspire to self-determination not civil rights
- We aspire to Biblical Justice not equality
- We aspire to our righteous monarchy not democracy
- We aspire to our covenant of the Ten Commandments not the U.S. Constitution.
- We aspire to Black Wall Street (Tulsa, OK 1921) not assimilation with racist.
- We aspire to our promise land not the American dream.

Moreover, the Bible is a testimony that the history of the Israelites is the greatest among all nations, and the fact that so many nations look to the Bible for guidance and instruction, this verifies that its righteousness as a socio-political, spiritual, cultural, medical, and even economic document is remarkable. Thus, many nations have gone to great extents to claim to be descendants of the original Israelites, *(e.g. Mormons, Russian Khazars, German Ashkenazi, and Edomites)* adopt our culture, and to tell our stories in Hollywood

## BYWORD

movies featuring Caucasians, capitalizing on the Israelite heritage of the descendant of slaves in the Americas. Such movies include *The Ten Commandments, Samson, The Passion of Christ etc.*

Moreover, I was blessed to have been educated by two wise Israelite men as my first teachers, **Priest Garth Bobb and Elder Troy Williams** in Columbia, Maryland. I thank all those who have demonstrated love and have supported me through my times of despair. I would like to acknowledge *Elder Shadrock, Chief Priest Patrick Stoute, Elder Michael Hinds, Priest Kevin, the Israelites Remnant in Christ Ministries, Yodit Niguse, Elder Claude* and *Beverly Clement Ferguson, Terence Joffrion, Janeiah Carpenter, Jarvis Hayes, Alexis Wingate, Ransom McNeil, Sharrieff Davis, Johnny Shelton Jr., Angela Hand-Gomez, Dr. James. F. Martin III*, who taught me *"being black is not a part-time job", my editor Michael ben Michael*, Aaron Young, Daren Duarte, Jerry Harmon, Uncle Author Williams, Terry Moreland, Sister Annie Moreland, Frank Plummer and many others I do not have space to mention herein.

The author would like to recommend three additional companion books **"The Truth, The Lie and The Bible" by Elder Shadrock "From Babylon to Timbuktu" by Dr. Rudolph R. Windsor, and "Post Traumatic Slave Syndrome" by Dr. Joy DeGruy.** The King James Version and the New International Version for all Bible scriptures served as the primary resources for *Byword*. Racial and national identity are significant because Israelite's are exclusively ordained to preach the Gospel and provide the counsel of the Most High (Psalm 147:19-20). All poetry created and written by Elder Makabi and Mark-Alan. *In honor of my father Oscar and in memory of my mother saint Ernestine I am the living testimony of*

## Elder Mark Makabi

*their righteous works!* All praises and glory to the God of Abraham, Isaac, and Jacob and his Christ!

### OSCAR'S TROWEL!
Mark-Alan

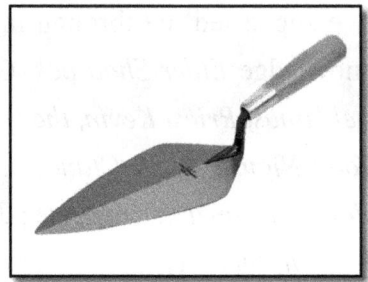

*The love of Oscar's trowel cornered the precious stone,*
*secured the **Diamonds** heart, hued the **Emerald** souls,*
*The heart of Oscar's trowel planted the tree of life,*
*Was guided by **Topaz royal** path, and treasured **Beryl's** laugh*
*The sacrifice of Oscar's trowel constructed*
*the bedrock of **Onyx** pebbles,*
*Healing **Sapphire** fragments, advocated **Amethyst** worth,*
*The faith of Oscar's trowel exalted **Jasper's** mountain,*
*The rhythm of Oscar's trowel produced*
*the soul of **Sardius** melodies,*
*The hand of Oscar's trowel imprints wisdom of understanding,*
*celebrating artisan thoughts, and showering the roots*
*of his monuments.*
*The power of Oscar's trowel insured*
***Carbuncle's** balance and elevation,*
***Agate's** equity and clarity, and the trust of **Ligure** cool flames,*

## BYWORD

*The memorial of Oscar's trowel confirms
the renaissance of his cornerstone.*

## CHAPTER 1
# FROM JERUSALEM TO JAMESTOWN
## "A Historical Overview of the Biblical Israelites"

It is unfortunate that the so-called "Black History" month, which takes place in February has been reduced to *"I have a dream"*, and is a part of the ongoing cycle of the *miseducation* of the *descendant of the Negro slaves* in the Americas. **Furthermore, to understand *miseducation*, we must understand that education is merely knowledge of self.** Education comes from Latin "educare", which means "to drive/draw out" or to extract in this case information, or what we call wisdom through experiences and revelations. Education is a means for people to gain control of their own thinking to provide for their basic needs. Furthermore, history should be a guide for us to remember how to conduct ourselves in the present in preparation for the future.

Nevertheless, our founding Hebrew fathers Abraham, Isaac, and Jacob of the Biblical nation of Israel are the direct ancestors of the slaves who came in ships that arrived in the Americas. Furthermore, our Israelite fathers arrived in ancient Egypt, (Mizraim) approximately 1876 B.C. This was the point in our Israelite history that Joseph was elevated from being a Hebrew slave to the most powerful man on the earth, only second to Pharaoh, as the Governor of ancient Egypt. In addition, Joseph's wisdom and power was rooted in his knowledge of his Israelite identity and love for the *God, and God's love of the patriarchs, Abraham, Isaac, and Jacob* whereas the Pharaoh of Egypt had to summon a slave in prison to save his powerful nation from famine, war, and other geopolitical crises.

The ancient Egyptians (Ham) showed our fathers their gratitude for saving their nation by enslaving and oppressing the Israelites; however, the Israelite prophet, Moses and high Priest, Aaron, Elders, Miriam, and Joshua led the nation of Israel to victory, defeating ancient Egypt with the power of faith/later, they made their Exodus to the Promise Land during the reign of the Egyptian Pharaoh Thutmose III (1486-1446 B.C.). However, the Israelites ongoing internal strife and disobediences led to their enslavement [punishment] *in Canaan, Babylon, Persia, Assyria and eventually America [New Egypt]* throughout their history. Moreover, during the process of time, the Israelites had great Israelite kings such as **King Saul, King David, King Josiah, and King Solomon;** however, their internal issues continued. This exposed them to the treachery of the Greeks, sons of Japheth. They arrived in 168 B.C. led by the Seleucid king, Antiochus IV. The pagan Greeks attempted to ***"Hellenize"*** our Israelite fathers; however, following the pacifist rebellion of the Ḥasidim (pious ones), the military power and genius of the *Maccabees (Israelites)* restored their independence between 167-144 B.C.

Later, our Israelite Messiah arrived to teach, unite, and ***save His people, Israel*** *(Matthew 1:21; 15:21-24) as the sacrificial Lamb and*

*King of Israel.* Nevertheless, between 70 and 135 A.D., the Roman General Titus destroyed our Israelite temple in northeastern Africa *(the so-called Middle-East)* and by 135 AD, the 12 tribes of Israel were scattered *(James 1:1).* The majority of the Israelites sought refuge in the land of Ham (Western Africa) were they built the Israelite empires of *Songhai, Gao,, Ghana, and Mali along with the great cities of Djenne and Timbuktu.* **Timbuktu was an Israelite center of Israelite propensity, civilization, and advanced educational progress. The Israelites that founded the University of Sankore, in Timbuktu.** Thus, because some Israelites converted to Islam and adopted Arabic names Timbuktu is refer to as an Islamic center of civilization; however, the truth is Timbuktu was an Israelite innovation in civilization. Moreover, the Israelites (not Christians) were being persecuted by the Gentile Romans in which many Israelites were thrown in stadiums with the lions, tigers, and bears to be killed for sport, burned at the stake, lynched, crucified on the cross, and beheaded (i.e. similar to the slaves and their descendants in the Americas). The Roman Catholics Christians took advantage of the fall of the Biblical nation of Israel by establishing their pagan philosophy of Christianity at the council of Nicaea in 324 AD, perverting the Israelite Bible to disguise their crude, redundant Socratic philosophy of control and deceit. When the Romans destroyed our Israelite temple and stole our Book of the Covenant *(the Bible)*, among many other things, (e.g. one of our national color Purple) their motive was to attempt to decipher the Israelites codes and advance their iniquitous agenda. However, since these heathens could not understand the Israelite Book of the Covenant, they developed an evil scheme to deceive the world and disguise their "witchcraft" in sheep's clothing by perverting the

## BYWORD

Bible. *For example, millions of Christians celebrate Christmas on December 25 as the birth of Jesus which is contrary to Israelites holy days (Jeremiah 10:1-4).* (KJV-Bible) "Hear ye the word which the Lord speaketh unto you, **O house of Israel: Thus saith the Lord, Learn not the way of the heathen,** and be not dismayed at the signs of heaven; for the heathen are dismayed at them. For the customs of the people are vain: **for one cutteth a tree out of the forest**, the work of the hands of the workman, with **the axe. They deck it with silver and with gold; they fasten it with nails and with hammers that it move not**." Nevertheless, the Israelites who successfully escaped the persecution of the Roman Catholics were met by the Ishmaelite's, Arabs Muslims, famous for their slogan *"convert or die."* **Woe unto the Ishmaelite's!**

Mohammed is a descendant of Ishmael he was illiterate and a servant to wealthy Israelite merchants. While Mohammed sojourned with Israelites, he learned about the Biblical covenant of the Israelites and his Ishmaelite heritage. In addition, when an Israelite woman named Khadijah's husband died, she married Mohammed. As Mohammed began to study his Ishmaelite heritage in the Bible (First Testament, Israelite Book of the Covenant) he adopted some of the Israelite spiritual and cultural customs; *(e.g. monotheism, abstain from pork, pray to the East, women cover their heads etc.)* although, Mohammed kept many pagan, Arab rituals and developed his new philosophy of Islam. The Moors (Israelites) sojourned to Iberia *(Spain and Portugal)* where they educated and *civilized the backwards European Gentile sons of Japheth* from their Dark Ages. The Moors introduce their advanced knowledge in *science, literature, religion, medicine, astronomy, geography, agriculture, engi-*

*neering, mathematics, fiancé, and philosophy between 900-1300 AD,* based on their keeping of the original Israelite scriptures and developing their knowledge of the world while honoring God, unlike the Christian Europeans who were denied information among their masses about the true nature of their religion under the Papacy and Roman Catholic dogma and doctrine.

There were Israelites that settled in Provence, France around 1066; many subscribed to the sense of nationalism and cultural perspectives of England under William the Conqueror and the Normans. However, few know that these same Israelite people (Moors) contributed, developed, and established Oxford University. Oxford University arose from the development and progressive history of the pre-Renaissance (European "rebirth") institution, Merton College in 1290 A.D. Merton was Oxford's first college; however, many European sources claim that Oxford began in 1096, some thirty years after the Norman Conquest of England. Merton was where Christians like Roger Bacon (1214-1292) became a student of the Israelites. Oxford University contains a *"Moses Hall" and Jacob's Hall"* named in honor of the Israelites and their extraordinary, educational contributions. In addition, the Israelites were the scholars that translated their history book, the First Testament and Second Testament of the Bible from their original Hebrew language into Greek, Latin, and later other European languages. This would later lead to the development of the King James Bible in 1612, centuries later.

Noting that the Israelites (Moors) and Ishmaelites (other Arabic Muslims) conquered much of lower Europe, many are not aware of the great contributions and accomplishments of the Israelites in Iberia. One such Israelite named **Tarik,** led the Israelites in Iberia.

# BYWORD

Iberia had become the central location where the European Gentile sons of Japheth began to redevelop their intellectual evolution at the waning of their Dark Ages (the age when the "dark" people of Earth led in all aspects of development and understanding). In addition to Tarik, *Abraham Ben Samuel Abulafia (1240-1292), Hasdai Crescas (1340-1410), Isaac Alfasi (1013-1103), and Levi B. Gershon (1288-1344) were powerful and influential Israelite leaders that maintained peace, commerce, freedom (even for Europeans in Grenada and Andulsia), and cultural development throughout the history of Israelite (Moorish) Iberia.* Unfortunately for the European Gentile sons of Japheth, there was an element that can only be identified as racial jealousy or dislike for the Israelites and their advances throughout the known world according to Europe. This led to ethnocentric philosophies (Eurocentric miseducation and racism) that did not embrace true wisdom but rather hid it in places like the Vatican, on one hand, while destroying aspects of this same knowledge during the expulsion of Jews (Israelite peoples) from Iberia and other regions of Europe. This forced exodus began during the Spanish Inquisition and later the "government-backed" removal of all non-European Christian individuals in Grenada and Andalusia in 1492 and would begin the upwelling of racism, deception, and lies that fed the unscrupulous claims that the European Gentile sons of Japheth were the originators of technology, philosophy, and cultural development established during the "Dark Ages" by the true originators of modern Europe, the (Biblical) Israelites. *(e.g. Congressman Steve King R-IA 4th District promoted the lie that the European Christians sons of Japheth contributed more to civilization on MSNBC July 2016)*

In 1473, King Ferdinand and Queen Isabella led the Christian

## Elder Mark Makabi

Inquisition whereas the Christians terrorizes and persecuted Israelites led by the malevolent Christian priest, Torquemada. King Ferdinand and Queen Isabella reclaimed and perverted the actual knowledge, culture, technology, and logic developed by the Moors (Israelites); this was part of the Reconquista or "reconquering" of Iberia and later much of Southern and Eastern Europe. The Age of Exploration that followed, placed Iberian nations in Europe (specifically Portugal and unified Spain) as the first modern nations to escape the European Dark Ages. The European Age of Exploration was based on maps created by Moors and other Abrabs Muslims (Israelites and Ishmaelites) such as Ibn al-Wardi **in the 13<sup>th</sup> century and Ahmad ibn Mājid in the 15<sup>th</sup> century. The wisdom and awareness of such a great land mass as the Americas was well-known among many Israelite scholars centuries before Cristobal Colon (Columbus) set sail for what he believed were uncharted islands off the coast of India (the Americas).**

**For clarification foreigners classified the entire Biblical nation of Israel as Hebrews or Jews; however, the Biblical Jews are Israelites from the tribe of Judah who came to the Americas with yokes of iron around their necks in slave ships and are not from Europe or Mount Seir.** All Jews are Israelites; yet, all Israelites are not Jews or are not from the tribe of Judah. Nevertheless as stated previously, on March 31, 1492, the Christian King Ferdinand and Queen Isabella issued a decree expelling Israelites from Spain by August 2, 1492, and in 1496, King Maneol issued his decree expelling all the Israelites from Portugal. In 1619, twenty Israelites captives were enslaved at Jamestown Virginia America.

## BYWORD

**Deuteronomy 28:68** "And the Lord shall bring thee into Egypt again with **ships**, by the way whereof I spake unto thee, Thou shalt see it no more again: and **there ye shall be sold unto your enemies for bondmen and bondwomen, and no man shall buy you**."

## CIMARRONES

**Historical Highlight:** The Cimarrones were valiant revolutionary men and women who took up arms and rebelled against their Spanish oppressors, later establishing a number of settlements of their own in Jamaica, which remain to the present day in the countryside. These Israelite slaves that escaped from plantations were classified as *Cimarrones (or Maroons in English under the British)* by their oppressors both Spanish and British in the 16th and 19th century. However, the Cimarrones developed and established their own independent communities, intermarried with the native Indians, and join forces with Sir Frances Drake under Elizabeth I (also known as "The Dragon" to the Spanish) to fight against the Spanish. The Cimarrones continue to be a great Israelite people of legends and national heroes of Jamaica and related nations in the Caribbean.

**Origins of name:** The Spanish assigned the name Cimarrones to the Israelites who rebelled and fled to the mountains, ergo cimarrones and the term maroon have been translated as "mountain ones" or mountain people" but also "fugitives" and "savages". The warped minds of the European-Spanish sons of Japheth kidnapped, enslaved, and oppressed the Israelites in the New World and then criminalized their activities to establish freedom through not only armed resistance, but simply flight to other parts of Jamaica and further into the Caribbean and the New World."

**Geography**: Jamaica, Panama, Central America

**Demographics**: A remnant of the 12 tribes of Israel scattered in the Americas.

***Clarifying the blur national, racial, and color lines***: *The so-called Cimarrones were transported in slave ships from West Africa to the Americas. Africa is a continent which has fifty-three (53) countries and was most likely named after a Phoenician prefix and Latin suffix, speaking the Spanish and English languages, and classifying their national and racial identity after the Spanish classification for fugitives.*

**Proverbs 3:31**: "Envy thou not the oppressor, and choose none of his ways."

**Cimarrones**: Spanish for "wild cattle," "runaway slave, "or "fugitives."

**Who's Your Father?** Who named Israelite's Cimarrones?

**In regards to your national identity, Cimarrones is a byword:** - Mockery

**Byword guides us back to our nation:**

    Biblical nation of Israel
    Race: Semitic
    Color of skin: Seven shades of brown
    Language: Hebrew
    Motherland: Jerusalem, Israel

## AFRO-NICARAGUANS

**Historical Highlight:** The atrocity of raping Israelite women during the Israelite captivity in the Americas under the Spanish resulted in the highly mix population of what is now Nicaragua. A shocking fact not taught in American and overall Western (Japhetic) schools is that slavery was abolished in 1821 in Nicaragua; however; it was re-established in 1854 by an American dictator *"William Walker"* who had the support of *American Presidents Franklin Pierce and James Buchanan.* These presidents were avid supporters of the Monroe Doctrine, which negated European colonial advances in the Americas, but invited U.S. "colonial interests" combined with Manifest Destiny in Central and South America.

The Israelites that were brought to work on the plantations and ranches in Nicaragua, Central America, and areas of the Caribbean were identify as Afro*mesitzo (Mexico under the Spanish), Afro-Antilleans (Caribbean under the Dutch), and Garifunas (Belize and Guatemala under the Spanish and British). These Israelites are interwoven into the very identity of Latin American culture, philosophy, and people. One of the great writers in Latin America was* **Ruben Dario Afromestizo (1867-1916), an Israelite poet**.

**Origins of name**: The most consistent story about the origin of the name Nicaragua is that the name was coined by the Spanish explorer, Gil Gonzalez Davilla, after the indigenous (Amerindian) Chief "Nicarao." Nicarao is a word from the Nahuatl language of the Aztecs. Nicaragua literally means, "The Waters of Nicarao", -agua, meaning "water".

**Geography**: Central America

**Demographics**: An estimated of 9% of the populations are Israelites *(descendant of slaves).*

***Clarifying the blur national, racial, and color lines***: The so-

*called Afro- Nicaraguans were transported in slave ships from West Africa to the Americas. Africa is a continent which has fifty-three (53) countries and was most likely named after a Phoenician prefix (Afar) and Latin suffix (ica), speaking the Spanish and English languages, and classifying their national and racial identity after the name of the land of an Amerindian Chief for which the Spanish named their colony (later nation).*

**Afro**: An abbreviation for African or referring to a hairstyle in the 1960s and 1970s in the United States. The afro reflected proactive self-awareness among the Israelite descendants of Negro slaves in the Americas.

**Nicaragua:** "Next to the water." Agua is Spanish for "water"

**Who's Your Father?** Who named Israelite's Afro-Nicaraguans?

**In regards to your national identity, Afro-Nicaraguan is a byword:** -Ridicule

**Byword guides us back to our nation:**

    Biblical nation of Israel

    Race: Semitic

    Pigmentation: Seven shades of blackness

    Language: Hebrew

    Homeland: Jerusalem, Israel

## AFRICANS

**Historical Highlight:** The original name of the African continent was Ham where the descendant of Ham settled after their language was confounded at the Tower of Babel (Mesopotamia Asia). Nevertheless, there are several theories as to the origin of how Africa received its name such as Africa derived from a tribe

# BYWORD

"**Aourigha**" *(pronounced "Afarika")*. However, the general consensus is the word Africa derives from a Phoenician *(Sidon)* word "**Afar**", which means **dust (and in some accounts "ancient)**, coupled with "**-ica**", a **Latin suffix** which was used to indicate "**land (of a people)**" versus "**terra**" meaning "**earth or soil**". The Romans combined these two words, "afar" and "-ica" into "Afar-ica", Africa, meaning "**Ancient Land of a People.**"

It was the "Latinized" influences on the name of Africa that followed after the Punic wars between Romans and Carthaginians or Punics (Phoenician colonists of ancient Libya and Tunisia (Tripolitania), Numidia, and Cyrenaica). Following the Second Punic War, the Roman General **Publius Cornelius Scipio** (236–183 BC) defeated Hannibal at Zama and claimed the land "Afar-ica" (a small area of the entire continent) and became **Scipio Africanus** or Scipio (conqueror of) Africa. From that point the land of Ham (the continent) was referred to by the Gentile sons of Japheth as Africa.

However, in a number of accounts there is evidence of the Israelites being recognized as "Black African" people. *The Igbo such as the Benei Gath "sons of Gad, son of Jacob", the Benei Zevulun, "Sons of Zevulun, son of Jacob", and the Benei Maneshsheh, "sons of Maneshsheh, son of Jacob"* are revered as true **Israelite (Biblical) people** not solely among Hamitic Africans but Japhetic Europeans.

**Origins of the name Africa**: The reasonable consensus is that the name derived `from the Phoenician word "**Afar**" meaning "**dust**" or "**ancient**" and the Latin suffix of the Romans "**-ica**" meaning "**land**" forming **Africa "Ancient Land of a People" or Aourigha.** However, remember that Phoenicians are sons of Ham by way of Canaan, and though they share many features as people of color with the sons of Shem, father of the Israelites, they are not Israelite people and thus their terms do not describe the Israelite people, accurately.

**Geography**: Africa.

**Demographics**: Over 1 billion people. Africa is a continent with fifty-three (53) countries, an estimate of 3000 ethnic tribes, and various languages. In addition, there are Israelites remnant scattered in the land of Ham Africa *(e.g. the Yoruba and Igbo of Nigeria, etc.)*

*Clarifying the blur national, racial, and color lines: The so-called Africans were transported in slave ships from West Africa to the Americas. Africa is a continent which has fifty-three (53) countries and was most likely named after a Phoenician prefix (Afar) and Latin suffix (ica), speaking various European languages, and classifying their national and racial identity after a continent named by European foreigners.*

**Phoenicians (Sidon):** The descendants of Ham are Hamites; however, not the "Negros" of the slave trade.

**Africa**: Phoenician prefix **"Afar"** attached with a Latin suffix **"-ica"**

**African:** The original name, **"Ham"**, means black, burnt, or dark (but not as a racial epithet or pejorative). This concept and classification was later adopted and generalized to describe among a diverse, unrelated number peoples among which the Israelites were associated based on similar physical features, but not common origin. The name of the land of Ham was reclassified to "Africa" and has been attributed to people recognized as "Hamites" or pre-colonial "Blacks" that were present in the Americas before the European sons of Japheth, starting with Columbus. These "Hamites" in the Americas were most likely *the Olmecs, Anasazis etc.*

**Who's Your Father?** Who told us we were Africans?

**In regards to your national identity, African is a byword:**
- Mockery

**Byword guides us back to our nation:**
>Biblical nation of Israel
>Race: Semitic
>Color of skin: Seven shades of brown
>Language: Hebrew
>Motherland: Jerusalem, Israel

## AFRO-LATINOS

**Latin**: Of or relating to the ancient Italic tribes from Vitulis "sons of the bull god" or "Vitela" ("Cowland") (more so at pasture). These tribes often said to be sons of Japheth were ruled for a time by the Etruscans, who were related to ancestors of the Hittites, Phoenicians, and later the Basque of the Pyrenees.

**Latin America:** Relating to people or countries speaking Romance languages that derived from Latin, speaking Spanish, Portuguese French, Italian, Romanian; however, there are some minorities of English, Dutch, Amerindian, Chinese, Indians of India, and Niger-Congo language speakers, thus the land is called, "Latin America".

**Geography**: Afro-Latinos live in 46 countries including the Caribbeans, North, South, and Central America.

**Demographics**: An estimate of 150 million Israelites *(descendant of slaves)* that identify as Afro-Latinos.

**Afro-Latinos**: Israelites of so-called African descent living in the Spanish and Portuguese-speaking nations of Latin America.

***Clarifying the blur national, racial, and color lines***: *The so-called Afro-Latinos were transported in slave ships from West Africa to the Americas. Africa is a continent which has fifty-three (53) countries and was most likely named after a Phoenician prefix and Latin suffix, speaking the Spanish, Portuguese, and English languages, and classifying their national and racial identity primarily based on simply speaking the Romance languages.*

**Latin**: Latin is a language of the ancient Etruscans who were related to the Hittites who were people of color, were considered Hamites (Black) who civilized the Italic and related tribes of Vitulis (Italy), specifically the city of Rome and thus the progenitors of the Roman Empire.

**Romance Languages:** The primary romance languages are Spanish, Portuguese, French, Italian, and Romanian. They are called "romance languages" because they originate from a language spoken by the Romans.

**Who's Your Father?** Who name Israelite's Afro-Black Latinos?

**In regards to your national identity, Afro-Latino is a byword:** - Ridicule

**Byword guides us back to our nation:**
- Biblical nation of Israel
- Race: Semitic
- Pigmentation: Seven shades of blackness
- Language: Hebrew
- Homeland: Jerusalem, Israel

# BYWORD

## MOORS

**Historical Highlight:** Contrary to popular opinion, the Moors who civilized Iberia *(Spain and Portugal from circa 700-1492 A.D.)* were predominately Israelites with an admixture of Ishmaelites, and Hamitic "African" people, who united under Islam. The Moors consist of diverse nations with high melanin or dark pigmentation (melanin, from the Greek melas for "black"). Many Israelites converted to Islam out of political pressure to avoid direct conflict with the Ishmaelite Arabs Muslims, who coined the threating phrase, *"convert or die."*

**Cabal al Tariq or Tarik** *(Rock of Gibraltar)* was a brilliant Israelite general who was known as a Moor. Whereas, Muhammad was illiterate and learned about his Ishmaelite heritage from the real Biblical Jews or Israelites *(ancestors of so-called Negro slaves in the Americas)*. In addition, Mohammed was a servant of a wealthy Israelite woman named Khadija (570-632 AD) and later became her husband.

**Origins of name**: The name Moor derives from Latin "maurus" in Greek "mauron." Moreover, the European sons of Japheth made the term "dark" or "black "which was associated with evil, despair, and dread, a synonym to describe the so-called "Negro" peoples of the world. The term Moor was most likely popularized during the European "Dark Ages" both darkness for European enlightenment, yet a time when the people of color such as the Israelites, Ishmaelites, and Hamites ruled the Mediterranean, West Africa, the so-called Near East, and Eastern Europe from 623 to 1492 A.D.

**Geography**: The Maghreb, Arabia, and Israel (Biblical).

**Demographics**: An estimate of individuals who identify as Moors of so-called African slave decedent in the Americas is not known.

# Elder Mark Makabi

***Clarifying the blur national, racial, and color lines***: *The so-called Moors were transported in slave ships from West Africa to the Americas. Africa is a continent which has fifty-three (53) countries and was most likely named after a Phoenician prefix (Afar) and Latin suffix (ica), speaking Arabic, Niger-Congo, Berber, Romance, and Germanic (English) languages, classifying their racial identity as a color which derives from words meaning "black" in the Greek and Latin languages.*

**Moors:** Black or very Dark, sometimes called the "blue men" in some Spanish social circles. The term "blue", unlike "black" among Europeans, was used to distinguish royalty as in "blueblood" **(i.e. Blue Bloods TV-Show)**; for it has been stated in many accounts that a number of Moors and related peoples ruled as leaders in Europe (i.e. MacDuff [sons of "Dubh", Gaelic for "black"] of Scotland and the legendary knight in the "Arthurian" legend, Sir Morien, son of Sir Agrovale and a Moorish princess. The Moors are said to have ruled successfully throughout Europe, specifically Western Europe, until the expulsion of the (Israelites), beginning in 1492. Moreover, eight years after this travesty of justice, 1500 A.D. was seen as the start of the so-called Modern Age beyond of the "Dark Ages" by the European Gentile sons of Japheth.

**The European Gentile sons of Japheth**: The carnal mind of Johann F. Blumenbach and Carl Von Linnaeus classified the races within the human species based on color of skin. Previous to this, due to the number of related peoples around the known world, ethnicity and culture preceded the concept of race. It is noted that "Black" Romans, both Israelite (Semitic) and so-called African (Hamitic) peoples living in the so-called empire, were prominent within Roman society based on citizenship and the political identity they accepted as "Romans". One notable "Mauros" or "Black" citizen among the Romans was St. Maurice or Moros of Thebes (Egypt).

**Who's Your Father?** Who named Israelite's moors?

**In regards to your national identity, Moors is a byword:**
- Mockery

**Byword guides us back to our nation:**
    Biblical nation of Israel
    Race: Semitic
    Color of skin: Seven shades of brown
    Language: Hebrew
    Motherland: Jerusalem, Israel

## AFRO-ANTILLEANS

**Historical Highlight:** Antilles refers the Latin words "ante" (before) or "anti" (against, more at opposite) compiled with the Portuguese word "ilha" meaning "island". This was the original reference to the Caribbean by the European sons of Japheth. The Antilles were seen as islands at the opposite end of the known world, thus the New World according to Europe.

**Origin of the name Antilles:** Antilles refers the Latin words "ante" (before) or "anti" (against, more at opposite) compiled with the Portuguese word "ilha" meaning "island".

The Antilles in some accounts refers to a legendary land (more than likely Atlantis), west of Iberia, known as Antilia or Antulia. The islands were referred to in medieval maps (more than likely based on Israelite and/or Hamitic seafarers' maps). These islands were a system of islands between the Canary Islands and India, according to the

European sons of Japheth. The Sea of Antilles and the Caribbean Sea were both used to describe the body of water that encumbers the area between Mexico and Mesoamerica, northern South America, southern North America, and the island nations therein.

**Geography**: Caribbean, a chain of islands divided by two parts, the Greater and Lesser Antilles.

**Demographics**: An estimate of individuals that identify as Afro-Antilleans in the Americas is not known.

**Indigenous Tribes**: (non-Israelite) The Arawaks, Tainos, Ciboneys Kalinagos, Galibis, Igneris and Lucayans.

**The Christian Catholics**: The Catholics played a malicious role in suppressing the Israelite culture and legitimizing the holocaust of slavery in the Americas.

*__Clarifying the blur national, racial, and color lines__: The so-called Afro-Antilleans were transported in slave ships from West Africa to the Americas. Africa is a continent which has fifty-three (53) countries and was most likely named after a Phoenician prefix and Latin suffix, speaking various European languages, classifying their national and racial identity after a Portuguese word that can be translated as the idiom, "the opposite end of the world".*

**Antilles:** A chain of island divided by two parts, the Greater Antilles and the Lesser Antilles. The greater includes Cuba, Jamaica, Puerto Rico, Hispaniola, Cayman, and Dominican Republic, and the Lesser Antilles include The Windward Islands (Martinique, St. Lucia, St. Vincent, the Grenadines, and Grenada) and the Leeward Islands (Virgin Islands, Dominica, Guadeloupe, Montserrat, Antigua, Barbuda, St. Kitts, Nevis, and Anguilla).

**Who's Your Father?** Who named Israelite's Afro-Antilleans?

# BYWORD

**In regards to your national identity, Afro-Antilleans is a byword: -** Ridicule

**Byword guides us back to our nation:**
>Biblical nation of Israel
>Race: Semitic
>Pigmentation: Seven shades of blackness
>Language: Hebrew
>Homeland: Jerusalem, Israel

## BLACK-BRITIANS

**Historical Highlight:** John Locke, whose philosophies were the foundation of the United States' so-called sense of democracy and freedom, was a primary supporter of the seizure and enslavement of the Israelites dwelling in West Africa in 1555.

In a trial in 1569 known as the Cartwright decision 1569, it was stated that "England air was too pure for slaves to breath." Cartwright was a slave owner. The slave was a man who was Russian (Russia is a Slavic nation, "Slavic", the root of the word slave). Cartwright beat the man so severely that it outraged onlookers. The man was freed; thus, it was deemed that English would not tolerate such abuse; however, the English sons of Japheth felt that British air was essentially too good for the "Hebrew slave." Yet, it was deemed sound in England if one bathed twice a year and threw human feces into the streets.

The Israelites taught many of the Gentile sons of Japheth that cleanliness is next to godliness and sanity through baptism and frequent bathing; however, most European nations did not embrace bathing until medical science during the 1800s stressed cleaning's hygenic benefits… Who was really unclean?

1618, a group of Englishmen began to enter the slave trade under "Company of Adventures." Sir John Hawkins was sponsored by the United Kingdom government under Mary I and later Elizabeth I to further the evil of Israelite in enslavement in the Americas. By 1672 the British dominated the Trans-Atlantic Slave trade through the *Royal African Company (1660-1752)*.

**Origin of Name Great Britain:** One historical etymological source traces the name to ***"Great Land of the Tattooed". The seafaring Greeks followed the journeys of the Phoenicians (Sidon) far before the Romans and described the inhabitants of the "British Isles" as the "Prettanoi"*** or "tattooed people". This is similar to the word "preto" or black in Portuguese. Another account is that "Brit" is a word meaning speckled and light colored as in one with freckles or various pigmentations. Yet, another source states that Brit is attributed to St. Brigid, a Celtic pagan goddess that was canonized by the Catholic Church. Thus Britain or Britannia means "Land of Brigid". "Brit" also is a word meaning "to break, divide, destroy, and even rule over" thus to "rule by division" and this is something the British sons of Japheth perfected among the people of color in the world.

One of the greatest notable Scots (Gaels, Celts) that was "Black" was Kenneth the Niger (as in the Nations Niger and Nigeria, meaning "black"). Kenneth III (Cináed mac Dubh, Kenneth son of (or the) Black Man) ruled southern Scotland as from 997-1005.

**Geography**: Europe: The United Kingdom of Britain and Northern Ireland.

**Demographics**: An estimated of over 1 million Israelites in the United Kingdom.

***Clarifying the blur national, racial, and color lines***: The so-

# BYWORD

*called Black Britains/Black British were transported in slave ships from West Africa to Europe. Africa is a continent which has fifty-three (53) countries and was most likely named after a Phoenician prefix (Afar) and Latin suffix (ica), speaking the English languages, and classifying their national and racial identity as a color and after the ethnicity of the English people.*

**Black:** Color relating to pigmentation from the word "bleh" meaning dark, sooty, smoke, or burnt.

**Britain:** Derives from the Greek "Prettanoi" and Celtic word "Brit" akin to the pagan Celtic goddess Brigid, who became St. Brigid under the so-called Roman Catholic Church. Britannia, Britain, means "Land of Brigid".

**Who's Your Father?** Who assigned you the name Black Britains, Black British, Afro-British, or Anglo Africans?

**In regards to your national identity, Black-Britain is a byword: -** Mockery

**Byword guides us back to our nation:**

    Biblical nation of Israel
    Race: Semitic
    Color of skin: Seven shades of brown
    Language: Hebrew
    Motherland: Jerusalem, Israel

## DOMINICANS

**Historical Highlight:** The Dominican Republic and Dominica are often confused with each other; yet, they are two completely different islands. In addition, the Dominican Republic speaks Spanish, while Dominica speaks English. **The Dominican Republic shares**

**an island with Haiti occupying three-eighths of the island Hispaniola in the west while the Dominica occupies the east.** The instability of the island began in 1492 with Columbus when he conquered and renamed the island *"La Espanola,"* or "The (New) Spain". However, Spain ceded the island to France in 1795. The Haitians conquered the island by 1804 under the leadership of Lieutenant Jean-Jacques Dessalines, initiated by the great Israelite general and military genius, *Toussaint L. Ouverture.* The war began in in 1791 against the French and ended thirteen years later.

The Spanish exploited uneasy ties between Haitians and their mixed or mulatto countrymen, who referred themselves as Dominicans from Santo Domingo, the name of the colony, named after the founder of the so-called Dominican order (St. Dominic). The Dominican revolts began in 1808 and undermined Haitian unity and rule; this led to the Spanish regaining control of "Spanish Haiti" in 1814. The Dominican Republic claimed independence from Haiti in 1821 and became an autonomous "protectorate" or new colony under Spain until 1844, when the nation claimed independence from Spain and became a completely sovereign nation under the dictator Pedro Santana.

Many Dominicans have a horrendous reputation of expressing disdain for all aspects of "Blackness" and their Israelite heritage. Some Dominicans practice extreme forms of self-hatred and propagating a sense of social and psychological slavery against darker members of their society (morenos). Many dark Dominicans like many Afro-Latinos are forced to claim their race as "white."

**Origins of name**: The land was populated by the Tainos/Arawaks before the mass murder Christopher Columbus arrived.

## BYWORD

Moreover, Bartholome Columbus originally named the island ***"La Neuva Isabela"*** after the Queen of Spain; however it was renamed ***"Santo Domingo"*** in honor of Santo Domingo Guzman or the so-called saint named Dominic the founder of the Dominican order.

**Geography**: The Island of Hispaniola in the Caribbean.

**Demographics**: An estimated of 84% of the populations are Israelites *(descendants of slaves)*.

***Clarifying the blur national, racial, and color lines***: The so-called Dominicans were transported in slave ships from West Africa to the Americas. Africa is a continent which has fifty-three (53) countries and was most likely named after a Phoenician prefix and Latin suffix, speaking the Spanish and English languages, and classifying themselves nationally and racially after the name of an island that was named after a Spanish Monk.

**Dominican Republic:** Named after "Santo Domingo Guzman."

**Who's Your Father?** Who named Israelite's Dominicans?

**In regards to your national identity, Dominican is a byword:** - Ridicule

**Byword guides us back to our nation:**

    Biblical nation of Israel

    Race: Semitic

    Pigmentation: Seven shades of blackness

    Language: Hebrew

    Homeland: Jerusalem, Israel

## Elder Mark Makabi

## KITTITIANS

**Historical Highlight:** The originally name of the island was *"Laimuiga"* before the arrival the European Gentile sons of Japheth; however, St. Kitts became a British territory in 1623. The skilled work of the Israelite slaves made this island exceptional wealthy as a sugar plantation colony. August 1, 1838 is emancipation day upon which the Israelite were legally, but not socially, free.

*"The Trial of "Quik" or "Quick"* was about an emancipated Israelite seaman, Quik who was a captain of a ship called the "Flora". Quik was commissioned by the Trinidad government to carry freed Israelites from St. Kitts to the southern Caribbean. However, Quick was charged for abduction of an unwed sixteen year-old girl. Quick stated he thought the girl was the wife of a ship hand. He was fined and imprisoned for six months. His trial was part of a series of judicial offenses against Israelite people in St. Kitts that eerily was identical to the legal actions in the United States by the American sons of Japheth (so-called white people, Southerners) against the sons of Shem, Israelites (so-called Negroes or "Black" Americans) during the horrendous "Jim Crow" era (c. 1890-1970).

**Origins of the name:** The original inhabitants where the Caribs Indians. After Christopher Columbus arrived in 1493, he renamed the island after his patron saint, the so-called saint named Christopher. However, in 1623, the English shortened the name to St. Kitts, which is their nickname for St. Christopher.

**Nation**: The Federation of St. Kitts and Nevis (Nevis from the Spanish *"Nuestra Señora de las Nieves* ", "Our Lady of the Snows") is an independent nation formed by two islands in the Leeward islands of the Lesser Antilles.

# BYWORD

**Geography**: The Caribbean.

**Demographics**: An estimated of over 90% of the populations are Israelites *(descendant of slaves)* this estimated includes Nevis.

***Clarifying the blur national, racial, and color lines****: The so-called Kittitians were transported in slave ships from West Africa to the Americas. Africa is a continent which has fifty-three (53) countries and was most likely named after a Phoenician prefix (Afar) and Latin suffix (ica), speaking the Spanish and English languages, and classifying their national and racial identity after an English nickname for Christopher.*

**St. Kitt:** Nick name for Christopher, who the European Gentile sons of Japheth presumptuously refer to as a saint. The Children of Israel are exclusively the saint or chosen of God (Psalm 148:14) according to the Bible.

**Who's Your Father?** Who named Israelite's Kittitians?

**In regards to your national identity, Kittitian is a byword:**
- Mockery

**Byword guides us back to our nation:**

    Biblical nation of Israel

    Race: Semitic

    Color of skin: Seven shades of brown

    Language: Hebrew

    Motherland: Jerusalem, Israel

## TOBAGONIANS

**Historical Highlight**: Tobago was a haven of hatred and war that augmented the Israelite Biblical Holocaust of slavery in the Americas. The island changed hands between the European sons of Japheth thirty three times between the Spanish, French, English, Dutch, and Swedish. Israelite freedom fighters were constantly lynched and continuous uprisings took place until 1834.

*"The Treaty of Amiens"* in 1802 gave the French control of Tobago; however an Israelite slave named *George Winchester* guided the English to the French fort and the French surrendered. In addition, George Winchester was paid, set free, and established his own company. Hence, economic development stemmed from Israelites captive agricultural and scientific skills in cultivation of sugar, rum, molasses, coconuts, cacao, and cotton.

The apprentice system was established, following so-called emancipation in August 1, 1834, where Israelite captives were bound to their former owners for up to four to six years (post-slavery, *involuntary* indentured servitude. *Eric Williams*, the Israelite Prime Minister of Trinidad and Tobago from 1962 to 1981 is considered the "father of the nation".

**Origins of name:** The name is believed to derive from the *Kalipunas* word for a smoking receptacle for tobacco. However, the Spanish re-named the *Kalipunas* Caribs which means "cannibal.

**Geography**: The Caribbean.

**Demographics**: An estimated of 58% of the populations are Israelites *(descendant of slaves)* this estimates includes Trinidad.

***Clarifying the blur national, racial, and color lines:*** *The so-called Tobagonians were transported in slave ships from West Africa to the Americas. Africa is a continent which has fifty-three (53) countries and was most likely named after a Phoenician prefix (Afar) and Latin suffix (ica), speaking the English languages, and classifying their national and racial identity after the name of the*

# BYWORD

*island which derives from the Kalipunas who the Spanish racially reclassified as Caribs or "cannibals".*

**Tobago:** A receptacle for tobacco or simply the substance "smoked".

**Who's Your Father?** Who named Israelite's Tobagonians?

**In regards to your national identity, Tobagonian is a by-word: -** Ridicule

**Byword guides us back to our nation:**
Biblical nation of Israel
Race: Semitic
Pigmentation: Seven shades of blackness
Language: Hebrew
Homeland: Jerusalem, Israel

## MY WALK, MY SHOES

*My walk, my shoes, my path, my blues, your discourse of diversity is converse, imitating my images expectations, your fears, your perceptions, My education, my responsibility, your miseducation, your manipulation, My truth, your lies, the lie confirms the truth; the devil is a liar, my laws, you're lawless, whose laws? The most High laws rules, My race, your disgrace, my color, your sin, my nigger, your name, my name, your nigga, my confusion, your illusion, your deception, my attention, my blues, your profit, my fears, your terror, my enslavement, your freedom, my captivity, your democracy, my freedom, my battle, my walk, my shoes,*

*My hood, your innovation, your suburb, my isolation, my wool,*

## Elder Mark Makabi

*your perm, my heroes, your image, my shame, my attitude, your defiance, my politics, my brother, my enemy, my sister, my foe, my family, my hoods, your Klan, my body, your physique, my hips, your figure, my natural hair, my spite, your models, my esteem, your icons, my admiration, my hate, your psychology, my shame, your movies, my story, your fame, my ignorance, my blame, my crimes, my consequences, my self-image, my dignity, my respect, my love-for-self, my walk, my shoes,*

*My savior, your god, my God, my ignorance, my Jesus, your beast Cesare Borgia, your civil rights, your control, my leadership, my forfeit, my Bible, your indoctrination, my values, your immorality, my love, your hate, my hate, your love, my integration, my contamination, my error, my spirituality, your sorcery, my Biblical heritage, your Edomite impostor, my lack of knowledge of self, my blame, my slave mentality, your treatment, my children, your education, your slaves my children, my nationality, your color, my classification, your color, my existence, your validation, my heritage, my identity, my nationality, my self-determination, my walk, my shoes,*

*My song, my rhythm, my dance, your imitation, my sex, my music, my creativity, my lips, my hips, your envy, my attitude, your defiance, my endowment, your anxiety, my walk, my talk, my swag, your mimic, your manipulation, my strategies, your inequities, my blessings, your curses, my gifts, my footsteps, your shoes, my language, my message, your misinterpretation, my mind, your control, your young, my rap, my control my glory, your theft, your lies, my stories, my gladiators, your icons, my Christ, your King,*

# BYWORD

*my eyes, your vision, my story, your script, my story, your movies, no culture, no history, no identity, my crime, your offenses, my hands, your remote, my tongue, your words, my creation, your profits, my shoes, your feet, my soul, your sale, my healing, my soul, my promises, my inheritance, my walk, my shoes,*

*My covenant, my breech, my self-destruction, your riches, my slavery, your profit, my slavery, my fall, your rise, my shame, my shame, your pride, my love, my pain, your gain, my sorrows, your joy, my cries, my rise, your destruction, my freedom, your captivity, my humility, my power, your weakness, His joy, my strength, your fall, my justice, my good, your evil, my evil, your good, my righteousness, your wickedness, my vengeance, your fears, my melanin, your sin, my melanin, your cursed, your leprosy, my color, your insecurity, my time, your end, my elect, your Babylon, my Zion, my separation, my salvation, my liberation, my walk, my shoes,*

*My race, your racism, my hate, my right, my rage, your sarcasm, my scars, your whip, my laugher, your agony, my scent, your stink, my God, your devil, your time, your end, my justice, your death, my fire, your stubble, my Armageddon, your burden, my wind, your tornadoes, my dry bones, my life, my resurrection, your demise, my eye, your eye, my stand, my ground, your hypocrisy, my sin, your racism, my wickedness, your laws, my reconciliation, your enslavement, my victory, your downfall, my reap, my reverse racism, my joy in the morning, my Black Messiah, my salvation, my respect, my retaliation, my reparations, my retribution, my redemption, my reward, my walk, my shoes.*

# CHAPTER 2
# THE SHAME OF SLAVERY
## "The Fall of the Biblical Nation of Israel"

**Deuteronomy 28:32 (KJV-BIBLE)**
"**Thy sons and thy daughters shall be given unto another people,** and thine eyes shall look, and fail with longing for them all the day long; and there shall be no might in thine hand."

# Byword

***The Israelite (Biblical) holocaust of slavery*** is a very emotional and offensive subject for the children of slavery; however, in the process of their healing, they must eat or drink those bitter herbs and take ownership of their holocaust of slavery in the Americas. This will end the ongoing cycle of their deplorable social, emotional, economic, physical, psychological, and spiritual conditions.

## WHAT IS THE SHAME OF SLAVERY?

*The psychological implications of the shame of the slavery; affected the horrendous self-image of the so-called Negros in the Americas.*

The shame of slavery is our curse of disobedience. We have been destroyed for lack of knowledge of self, rejecting knowledge, our self-hate, our division, emotional, and physical lynching, the injustices, our oppression, the rape of our sisters and mothers, the castrating of our fathers and brothers. The shame of slavery is our transgressions, family dysfunction, the sins of our Israelite fathers, abandoning our family and cultural values, our rage, our discrimination, racism, our free labor, building a house and not living in it, no reparations, no redemption, no retribution, and no recognition for our extraordinary contributions, our abduction, our *miseducation*, the middle passage holocaust, our inferiority and shades of color complex, our beautiful black skin, our beautiful brown color, our melanin, our beautiful full lips, our good wooly hair, our beautiful big flat noses, our misunderstanding of being created in the image and likeness of the most High.

The shame of slavery is the centuries of injustices, Rosewood, Black Wall Street, the slave stock market, slave blocks, race riots,

# ELDER MARK MAKABI

our burnings at the stake, our holocaust, Emmett Till, police brutality, the Grand Jury sanctions of cold-blooded police murders of our sons and brothers, Judas kissers, the rape of our boys by wicked homosexuals pedophiles, the American white-trash minstrels, the slave trade, our humiliation, our Bible and their Christian indoctrination, suppression of our natural God-given Biblical righteous response of anger, rage, hate, revenge, retribution, reparation, redemption, revolution, and retaliation for the injustice.

The shame of slavery is believing in the hypocrisy of democracy, our denial, the selling of our souls for civil rights, rape of our children and women *(i.e. psychological, social, spiritual, and moral)*, our pain, our hardship, our psychological scars, our spiritual, mental, social, and emotional disorders, the ghetto, our division, the abortion rate in our communities, our fatherless homes, our gangs, our distrust of each other, the murder rate among our brothers.

The shame of slavery is our special education rate among black boys, our preschool to prison channel of our black boys, our current 60% prison population, our glorification, support, popularization, and embracing of the "nigger" affirming that we're nonpersons, and our dishonor of our father and mother. The shame of slavery is our entertainment buffoonery, our sagging pants, our worshiping of wood and stone, the disrespect of our elders, our single mothers, our women heading the household, police killings, the stranger in you, cotton picking history, our failed marriages, and our family division.

The shame of slavery is being without sanctuary, our emotional, spiritual, and cultural integration, our unemployment rate, our drug and alcohol abuse, O.J. , The yokes around our necks and minds, our floggings, not establishing the memorial of our Israelite holocaust of slavery museum, not establishing the real Rock and Roll museum, the house negro, the Willie Lynch scenario, and becoming a byword. The shame of slavery is becoming a slave in 1619, the 1793 fugitive slave act, the 1857 Dred Scott decision, mental slavery, powerlessness, our 40 acres and a mule?, being attack by dogs and sprayed by water hoses, supporting the historically racist Democratic political party (also known as the Dixiecrats), perming our wooly and nappy hairs, worshiping the stone of Islam, the wood of Christianity, and the image of the beast Cesare Borgia as Jesus, the Zong 142, our Hellenization , our colonialism, our slaves names, cultural practices, and spirituality that is contrary to our Biblical family values such as the abomination of homosexuality, feminist, abortion, so-called liberalism, conservatism, socialism, celebrating the feast of the winter solstice on December 25, observing of a pagan customs Easter, Kwanza, Hanukah, Ramadan, and denied to speak in our original Hebrew language.

*The shame of slavery is the 16$^{th}$ street Baptist church bombing, the Charleston, SC Nine Massacre (2015), Roof, the Scottsboro boys, the Amistad trial, the Compromise of 1850, Anthony Johnson (1621), Brown v. Board of Education (1954), assassination of Medgar Evers, Malcolm X, and Dr. Martin L. King, Jim Crow, the Tuskegee experiment, Sean Bell, Korryn Gaines, Alton Sterling, Jamar Clark, Tamir Rice, Philando Castile, Sandra Bland, Trayvon Martin, Sherrice Iverson, Eric Gardner, Michael Brown, James Byrd Jr., Tyisha Miller, Garnett Paul Johnson Jr., Plan Parenthood, (1960) Ruby Bridges, the Jena Six, and the Little Rock Nine.*

The shame of slavery is our 100 years of lynching, [100 Years of Lynching] *Pierce city mob August 21, 1901, Negro Tortured to*

## Elder Mark Makabi

*Death by Mob of 4000,* **Girls in Teens Take Part in Raid on Funeral Home Bainbridge GA, May 25, 1937 "Because police had killed Willie Reid, Twenty-four, Negro, alleged murderer and rapist, a mob couldn't lynch him. But they broke into a mortuary, hauled his body off to the ball park and there burned it."** *1902, Negro Dragged from Cell and Tortured to Death June 8, 1902, Negro Murder Suspect Burned June 23, 1903, Negro Woman Pleading Innocence Lynched as Child Poisoner July 27, 1903, Lynched Negro and Wife were fist Mutilated February 8, 1904, Negro Lynched After Receiving Supreme, Court Reprieve March 20, 1906, 15 Negroes Are Shot Down August 1, 1910, Angry Miner Lynch Negro October 12, 1910, 1912, Negro Hanged to Trestle, a mob estimated at 2000 men, hanged and shot several bullets were then fired into his body August 12, 1913, Lynched Negro Cleared August 28, 1913, Lynched Negro Cleared.* **Heart and Genitals Carved from Lynched Negroes Corpse Kountze Texas December 8, 1933,**

The shame of slavery was the fall of our Biblical nation of Israel. This resulted in the wrath of the God of Israel. He poured out on the Israelites for their transgressions and as an example for all nations of the earth to learn, understanding, and considered there will be a Judgment Day. Woe to America!

**On December 2, 1859, Brown wrote:**

"I, John Brown, am now quite certain that the crimes of this guilty land will never be purged away but with blood. I had, as I now think, vainly flattered myself that without very much blood shed it might be done."

## BYWORD

*The Israelite (Biblical) Holocaust of
Slavery in the Americas Memorial.
Never Forget, Never Again!*

### PUERTO RICANS

**Historical Highlight:** The Israelites *(aka Moors)* accompanied the Spanish conquistadors to the island were the Tainos natives lived. The Tainos were nearly extinct due to enslavement and the diseases that the European Gentile sons of Japheth brought to the island. Moreover, Puerto Rico has a rich Israelite history and cultural heritage that includes many slave insurrection (**Grito de Lares, Ponce, Vega Baja conspiracies**), kings, navigators, explorers, educators, and military heroes *Ricardo Alegria, Juan Garrido, Pedro Mejias, Rafael Cordero, and captain Miguel Henriquez.* The Israelite captives made extraordinary contributions to the economic, social, cultural, political, and spiritual development of Puerto Rico.

**Origins of the name:** Christopher Columbus named this island "San Juan Bautista (after the Israelite saint John the Baptist) during his second voyage in 1493. However, the island named was renamed "Puerto Rico" (Rich Port). San Juan became the name of the current capital of the Spanish colony, now U.S. territory.

**Geography**: The Caribbean

**Demographics**: An estimated of 11.3% of the populations are Israelites *(the descendants of slaves)*.

***Clarifying the blur national, racial, and color lines***: *The so-called Puerto Ricans were transported in slave ships from West Africa to the Americas. Africa is a continent which has fifty-three (53) countries and was most likely named after a Phoenician prefix (Afar)* *and Latin suffix (ica), speaking the Spanish and English languages, and classifying their national and racial identity after the name of the island that derives from Spanish words for wealth (being rich... off the labor of slaves), and the color black.*

**Afro Black Puerto Ricans** – All Puerto Ricans are not Israelites however, Puerto Ricans that are the descendant of slaves are considered Israelites.

**Puerto Rico**: Spanish for "Rich Port."

**Who's Your Father?** Who named Israelite's Puerto Ricans?

**In regards to your national identity, Black Puerto Rican is a byword:** - Ridicule

**Byword guides us back to our nation:**
    Biblical nation of Israel
    Race: Semitic
    Pigmentation: Seven shades of blackness
    Language: Hebrew
    Motherland: Jerusalem, Israel

## CAPE VERDEANS

**Historical Highlight:** Colonized by the Portuguese, Cape Verde was a slavery port of West Africa in the 1700s where Israelite captives were sold to the Spanish, French, and English to build their colonies in the Americas and the Caribbean. Moreover, Cape Verde became an important watering station and sugar cane plantation. In addition, *Alfonos Nino* was a great Israelite scientist and navigator that sailed with Columbus when they sailed to the Cape Verde region. Therefore, we Honor and remember *"The Cardiff Docks"*. There is a Cape Verdean community in Cardiff, Wales.

# BYWORD

**Origins of the name:** Named after Cap-Vert which is a cape in Senegal and the westernmost point of Africa. The name derives from the Portuguese "Cabo Verde" which means "Green Cape".

**Geography**: West Africa, consisting of 10 islands

**Demographics**: An estimated of 96% of the populations are Israelites *(descendants of slaves)* including Creoles (intermarriage between the Israelites and Europeans).

***Clarifying the blur national, racial, and color lines***: *The so-called Cape Verdeans were transported in slave ships from West Africa to the Americas. Africa is a continent which has fifty-three (53) countries and was most likely named after a Phoenician prefix and Latin suffix, speaking the Portuguese or English language, and classifying their national and racial identity from a Portuguese word.*

**Cape Verde** – "green cape."

**One Drop Rules! Negro Blood** Historically, it was custom for mulattos or creoles to deny their Negro blood to improve their social and economic status in the Americas. However, the European Gentile sons of Japheth understood that one drop of Negro blood was superior and dominant. Therefore, they classify a person with one drop as a Negro. Nevertheless, in the near future, it will be popular for numerous nations to start claiming that they have Negro blood.

**Who's Your Father?** Who named Israelite's Cape Verdeans?

**In regards to your national identity, Cape Verdean is a byword:** - Mockery

**Byword guides us back to our nation:**
    Biblical nation of Israel

# ELDER MARK MAKABI

Race: Semitic
Color of skin: Seven shades of brown
Language: Hebrew
Homeland: Jerusalem, Israel

## AMERICO-LIBERIANS

**Historical Highlight:** Liberia is a nation whose origin lies in a paradox within United States history. The American Colonization Society (ACS) was founded in 1817 and was committed to the re-settlement of the ex-slaves outside the United States. In addition, the ACS used private funds donated by wealthy American sons of Japheth contributors to "purchase" land in West Africa and recruited freed-slaves or freedmen. Moreover, the first settlers arrived in 1821; however, the American sons of Japheth who were appointed by the ACS governed the colony in the early years. Nevertheless, in 1847 the ex-slaves declared their independence and became a sovereign republic. Joseph Jenkins Roberts was the first and seventh Israelite President of Liberia (1848 and 1856). Moreover, the Israelites *(Americo Liberians)* ruled Liberia for 133 years (1847-1980). Currently, Liberia is struggling to reclaim greatness, years of civil war throughout the region in the latter half of the 20th century were between Americo-Liberians and native peoples that had been present long before the Trans-Atlantic Slave Trade.

**Origin of the name:** Derives from the Latin "liber" meaning "free"

**Geography:** Liberia, West Africa

**Demographics:** an estimated of 4-5% of the populations are Israelites *(the descendants of slaves)*

# BYWORD

*Clarifying the blur national, racial, and color lines*: The so-called Americo-Liberians were transported in slave ships from West Africa to the Americas. Africa is a continent which has fifty-three (53) countries and was most likely named after a Phoenician prefix (Afar) and Latin suffix (ica), speaking English, and classifying their national and racial identity from a word that derives from a prefix based on the name of an Italian cartographer and a suffix that is a Latin word for "freedom".

**Prefix Americo:** Amerigo Vespucci an Italian explorer
**Liberia:** Derives from the Latin "liber", meaning "free"
**Americo-Liberian:** "Amerigo-free"
**Who's Your Father?** Who named Israelite's Americo-Liberians?
**In regards to your national identity, Americo-Liberian is a byword:** - Ridicule
**Byword guides us back to our nation:**

    Biblical nation of Israel
    Race: Semitic
    Pigmentation: Seven shades of blackness
    Language: Hebrew
    Motherland: Jerusalem, Israel

## BLACK-CARIBS

**Historical Highlight:** The common version of the origins of the **"Black Carbis"** is that in 1635, two Spanish ships carrying Israelite captives shipwrecked on the island of St. Vincent. These first slaves escaped from their bondage and arrived on the island as freemen, later encountering the Kalipunas Amerindians. Initially there were conflicts between the Israelites and Kalipuna Amerindians; however, they learned to dwell together and intermarried, thus creating the "Black Caribs."

**Origin of the name**: The Spanish called the Kalipuna Amerindians "Caribes" (Caribs) which means cannibals and that is the word from which "Caribbean" is derived.

**Geography**: Belize, North America, South and Central America, and the Caribbean.

**Demographics**: an estimated of over 250,000 Israelites (*Black Carbis descendants of slaves)*

*Clarifying the blur national, racial, and color lines:* *The so-called Black Carbis were transported in slave ships from West Africa to the Americas. Africa is a continent which has fifty-three (53) countries and was most likely named after a Phoenician prefix and Latin suffix, speaking the Garifuna language, and classifying their national and racial identity as a color and the Spanish pejorative of the Kalipuna Indians, referring to them as cannibals.*

**Black:** Color

**Caribs:** Meaning "cannibals"

**Black Carbis**: Black Cannibals

**Who's Your Father?** Who named Israelite's Black Caribs?

**In regards to your national identity, Black-Caribs is a byword:** - Mockery

**Byword guides us back to our nation:**
    Biblical nation of Israel
    Race: Semitic
    Color of skin: Seven shades of brown
    Language: Hebrew
    Homeland: Jerusalem, Israel

## BYWORD

## GUADELOUPEANS

**Historical Highlight:** A Dutch man who owned over 100 Israelite slaves provided the earliest record of the Israelite arrival in Guadeloupe; the year was 1654. The area was colonized by the French and populated by the Israelites. In Guadeloupe, Israelite slaves were permitted to have weapons in alliances with the French to fight against the British. Later, there was a slave revolt in which Israelites refused to return to slavery. In one instance, the slaves went into a gun powder warehouse and remained inside when the gun powder exploded. Furthermore, there were two great Israelites chiefs *"Chatoyer" and "Duvalier"* (so-called Black Caribs) that defended their land against the British. Among the Israelites that dwelled in Guadeloupe, Joseph Boulogne was a popular classical composer. Guadeloupe is not a sovereign nation but remains a French territory.

**Origin of the name**: Following the mass murder of island natives, Christopher Columbus named this island after the Spanish Virgin "Santa Marie de Guadalupe".

**Geography**: Caribbean, St. Bart is a dependent island of Guadeloupe.

**Demographics**: An estimated of 90% of the populations are Israelites *(descendants of slaves)*

*Clarifying the blur national, racial, and color lines: The so-called Guadeloupeans were transported in slave ships from West Africa to the Americas. Africa is a continent which has fifty-three (53) countries and was most likely named after a Phoenician prefix and Latin suffix, speaking French, and classifying their national and racial identity after a named by an Italian after the Israelite, the Virgin Mary, who was a woman of color.*

## ELDER MARK MAKABI

**Guadeloupe:** The Virgin "Santa Marie de Guadalupe." The Virgin Mary was an Israelite woman (Black woman) and Saint.

**Who's Your Father?** Who named Israelite's Guadeloupeans?

**In regards to national identity, Guadeloupeans is a byword:** - Ridicule

**Byword guides us back to our nation:**
    Biblical nation of Israel
    Race: Semitic
    Pigmentation: Seven shades of blackness
    Language: Hebrew
    Motherland: Jerusalem, Israel

### AFRO-BELIZEANS

**Historical Highlight:** previously referred to as called the British Honduras, Belize was originally populated by the Mayans. The Mayans were the indigenous population before the Spanish arrived and drove the Mayans to remote rural areas. Furthermore, the Spanish and British colonists brought Israelite slaves to develop and managed the timber industry in the area, specifically for mahogany. The Israelite slaves revolted in 1773 and many Israelites slaves fled for freedom to the Yucatan peninsula.

**Origin of the name:** Belize derives its name from one of two historical sources: Maya root words Belix meaning "muddy waters" or the surname of the Scottish buccaneer Peter Wallace, during the seventeenth century.

**Geography:** Central America

**Demographics:** An estimate of 37% of the population are Israelites **Creoles** (the intermarriages of the Israelites and British) and the **Garifuna** (*Black Caribs.*)

***Clarifying the blur national, racial, and color lines****: The so-called Afro-Belizeans were transported in slave ships from West Africa to the Americas. Africa is a continent which has fifty-three (53) countries and was most likely named after a Phoenician prefix (Afar) and Latin suffix (ica), speaking various languages of Creole (Pidgin English) English, Spanish, and classifying their national and racial identity from a name that most likely derives from the Mayan language.*

**Afro**: An abbreviation for African or referring to a hairstyle popular during the 1960s and 1970s among people of color, promoting Israelite heritage, glory, and freedom in the Americas..

**Belize: from the** Mayan root "Belix".

**Who's Your Father?** Who named Israelite's Afro-Belizeans?

**In regards to your national identity, Afro-Belizean is a byword:** - Mockery

**Byword guides us back to our nation:**
    Biblical nation of Israel
    Race: Semitic
    Color of skin: Seven shades of brown
    Language: Hebrew
    Homeland: Jerusalem, Israel

## AFRO-ARUBANS

**Historical Highlight:** Why has the history of Israelite slavery in Aruba been ignored in their educational institutions? Why is there a lack of general knowledge of slavery in Aruba? Furthermore, Israelite slavery existed in 1715 for four years and was re-introduced in 1800 to1863. In 1849, approximately 20% of the population consists of Israelite captives. Slavery was completely abolished in 1863. Over 500 Israelites received their freedom.

**Origin of the name**: Aruba derives its name from one of the two historical sources: Derives from the Arawaks "Oibubai" meaning "Guide" or the Spanish explorer "Alonos de Ojeda" named the island ""Oro Hubo" meaning "Presence of Gold" which translates "there was gold."

**Geography**: Caribbean

**Demographics**: 80% are intermarriages of Israelites (*descendants of slaves),* the European Gentile sons of Japheth, and Amerindians.

*Clarifying the blur national, racial, and color lines:* *The so-called Afro-Arubans were transported in slave ships from West Africa to the Americas. Africa is a continent which has fifty-three (53) countries and was most likely named after a Phoenician prefix and Latin suffix, speaking Dutch and Papiamento (a creole language), and classifying their national and racial identity form a name that most likely derives from the Arawaks.*

**Aruba**: Guide or presence of Gold.

**Who's Your Father?** Who named Israelite's Afro-Arubans?

**In regards to your national identity, Afro-Aruban is a byword** - Ridicule

**Byword guides us back to our nation:**
    Biblical nation of Israel
    Race: Semitic
    Pigmentation: Seven shades of blackness

# BYWORD

Language: Hebrew
Motherland: Jerusalem, Israel

## BERMUDIANS

**Historical Highlight:** Contrary to popular opinion the European Gentile sons of Japheth elite understood the talent and superior ability of the Israelites scientific, medical, architecture, mechanical, nautical, engineering, mathematic, and agricultural skills to build their colonies. The holocaust of slavery began in 1616 under Governor Daniel Tucker who instructed his sea captain Mr. Wilmott to secure the diving expertise of the Israelites to dive for pearls. In addition, Bermuda became a British colony in 1684 and chattel slavery was founded on the propaganda. The propaganda promoted the lies that the Israelites captives were intellectually inferior and brutes. This was rationalization and justification for the barbaric treatment of the Israelites in the Americas. The European Gentile sons of Japheth's savage and inhumane treatment of the captives led to many Israelite revolts. The Mary Prince (1788) story. The account was about an Israelite family that was separated on the auction block during a slave trade. Mary Prince received regular abuse by her barbaric, Caucasian owner; he raped her and tied her up to a ladder to give her 100 lashes. The brutality within this historic account contributed to the abolishment of slavery in Bermuda. The abolishment took place on August 28, 1833.

**Origin of the name**: Name after the Spanish sea captain "Juan de Bermudez" who sighted the island in 1503.

**Geography**: Caribbean.

**Demographics**: 63% of the population are Israelites *(the descendants of slaves)*

# ELDER MARK MAKABI

*Clarifying the blur national, racial, and color lines:* The so-called Bermudians were transported in slave ships from West Africa to the Americas. Africa is a continent which has fifty-three (53) countries and was most likely named after a Phoenician prefix (Afar) and Latin suffix (ica), speaking English, and classifying their national and racial identity after the surname of a Spanish captain.

**Bermuda**: Named after a Spanish captain "Juan de Bermudez."

**Who's Your Father?** Who named Israelite's Bermudians?

**In regards to your national identity, Bermudian is a byword:** - Mockery

**Byword guides us back to our nation:**
 Biblical nation of Israel
 Race: Semitic
 Color of skin: Seven shades of brown
 Language: Hebrew
 Homeland: Jerusalem, Israel

## DOMINICA

**Historical Highlight:** Dominica and the Dominican Republic are completely two different Caribbean islands. Dominica is an English speaking island in the Eastern Caribbean while the Dominican Republic speaks Spanish and shares an island, Hispaniola, with Haiti in the western Caribbean. Contrary to popular beliefs the Israelites captives were not exclusively cotton pickers; they brought various superior science, medical, agricultural, legal, cultural, and musical skills and abilities to build the Americas (i.e. Moors of Iberia). However, the anti-Semitic institution of racism limited their opportunities to excel. The native Arawaks were overthrown by the Caribs in the 14$^{th}$ century. Following Columbus' arrival in 1493 and the census riot, the Israelite captives and Kalipunas *(so-called Caribs)* as a united front began a series of revolts against the Europeans Gentile sons of Japheth. Three great Israelite captives were elected to the legislative branch of government, following the abolition of slavery in 1833. Nevertheless, in 1838 Dominica was the first and only British Caribbean colony to have an Israelite-controlled legislature in the 19th century.

**Origin of the name**: The popular historical account is that Christopher Columbus named the island "Dominica" because he landed there on a Sunday (or "domingo" in Spanish).

**Geography**: Caribbean.

**Demographics**: 80% of the population are Israelites *(the descendants of slaves)*

*Clarifying the blur national, racial, and color lines: The so-called Dominicans were transported in slave ships from West Africa to the Americas. Africa is a continent which has fifty-three (53) countries and was most likely named after a Phoenician prefix (Afar) and Latin suffix (ica), speaking the English and <u>Antillean Creole</u> (a French-based Creole) languages, and classifying their national and racial identity after the name of the island which an Italian named for Sunday.*

**Dominica**: From the Medieval Latin "Dics Dominica" meaning Sunday.

**Who's Your Father?** Who named Israelite's Dominicans?

**In regards to your national identity Dominican is a byword:** - Ridicule

**Byword guides us back to our nation:**
Biblical nation of Israel

# Elder Mark Makabi

Race: Semitic
Pigmentation: Seven shades of blackness
Language: Hebrew
Motherland: Jerusalem, Israel

## NEVISIANS

**Historical Highlight:** Nevis was a popular port for the Trans-Atlantic Slave Trade for English and Dutch on their way to the Americas (1675-1730). Sugar cane became the source of economic wealth. There were pro-slavery, "Christian" mobs at *Charlestown Methodist Chapel* during a battle in 1802. Later, the Israelite captives would battle the French while defending their families. Slavery was abolished on August 1, 1834. The Gentile European criminals were paid compensation for their crimes while the enslaved Israelites received nothing for 200 years. Nevis was united with St. Kitt and Anguilla in 1971 and on September 19, 1983 they became an independent nation.

**Origin of the name**: Pre-Columbian name was "Qualie" which translates to "Land of Beautiful Waters." However, Nevis is derived from the Spanish name *"Nuestra Senora De Las Nieves"* which means *"Our Lady of the Snows."* However, who named the island is unknown.

**Nation**: The Federation of St. Kitts and Nevis is an independent nation formed by two islands in the Leeward Islands of the Lesser Antilles.

**Geography**: Caribbean.

**Demographics**: An estimated of over 90% of the populations are Israelites *(descendants of slaves)* this estimated includes St. Kitts.

# BYWORD

***Clarifying the blur national, racial, and color lines:*** *The so-called Nevisians were transported in slave ships from West Africa to the Americas. Africa is a continent which has fifty-three (53) countries and was most likely named after a Phoenician prefix and Latin suffix, speaking English and French, and classifying their national and racial identity after the name of the island that derives from the word for snow in Spanish.*

**Nevis**: Our Lady of the Snows

**Who's Your Father?** Who named Israelite's Nevisians?

**In regards to your national identity, Nevisian is a byword:**
- Mockery

**Byword guides us back to our nation:**

    Biblical nation of Israel

    Race: Semitic

    Color of skin: Seven shades of brown

    Language: Hebrew

    Homeland: Jerusalem, Israel

## 12 HEALING LEAVES!

*Israelite emancipation; healing of the nations*
*Slavery reparations; healing of the nations,*
*Byword education, healing of the nations,*
*Racism eradication, healing of the nations,*
*Righteous indignation, healing of the nations,*
*Truth edification, healing of the nations,*
*The slaves' self-determination, healing of the nations,*
*Slavery memorialization, healing of the nations,*
*The covenant reconciliation, healing of the nations,*

# Elder Mark Makabi

*Anti-abominations, healing of the nations,*
*Dry bones regeneration, healing of the nations,*
*The 12 tribes' reunification, healing of the nations,*
*Israel's sanctification, healing of the nations,*
*Promise land restoration, healing of the nations*
*Levites purification, healing of the nations,*
*Temple rededication, healing of the nations,*
*The Passover celebration, healing of the nations,*
*Abib New Year proclamation, healing of the nations*
*Jubilee personification, healing of the nations,*
*Sabbath rejuvenation, healing of the nations,*
*Israelite consecration, healing of the nations,*
*Colonization extermination, healing of the nations*
*Demonization of miseducation, healing of the nations*
*Israel's legal obligation, healing of the nations,*
*Israel's retaliation, healing of the nations,*
*Edom's annihilation, healing of the nations,*
*Israel's salvation, healing of the nations,*
*The stranger's oblations, healing of the nations,*
*Negroes to Israel transformation, healing of the nations*
*2019 calculation, healing of the nations,*
*Romans 11:26 expectations, healing of the nations,*
*The Negroes are Israelites revelation, healing of the nations,*
*Holiness preparation, healing of the nations,*
*New Jerusalem foundation, healing of the nations,*
*Israelites liberation, healing of the nations,*
*Revelation 22:2 application, healing of the nations,*

## CHAPTER 3
# BAPTIZED INTO THE RELIGION OF SLAVERY!
## "Reclaiming the Religious Identity of the Children of Slavery"

What role did the Bible, religious ideology, and Christian and Islamic philosophies play in the enslavement of the Israelites? Between 70 and 135 A.D. the **Israelite diaspora** fled from Jerusalem into Africa to escape Roman persecution. Many settled in West Africa and established the kingdoms of Ghana, Mali, Mali's great city of Timbuktu, and Songhai. Thus, the Israelite religion and cultural practices continued in West Africa. However, the Israelites religious identity was reclassified under Niger-Congo African religious beliefs, such as Vodou (voodoo or "ghost/ancestor worship", worship of the Orishas, pagan gods) or Obeah (folk magic) by the Christian, European sons of Japheth invaders.

Nevertheless, some of the West African Israelite religious and cultural practices predate the colonial Christianization period. These practices include "**circumcision of the males,**" "**offering-up**"or presenting the child before the God of Israel *(e.g. in the scene from **Roots** (1977) were the father of Kunta Kinte raises his son above his head* *is "offering up our children unto to the Lord when naming our children." There was a strict* **"belief in a supreme God, monotheism," The division of 12 tribes whereas the priesthood belonging to one tribe**, honoring *(not worshiping)* **our father and mother** *(i.e. elders and ancestors)*, *polygamy, concubines, a Sabbath day of rest, praise and worship included music and dancing which was vital to our religious and cultural practices, and balancing spirituality with nature. For instance, the Israelite New Year celebrations begin in spring (Abib) which is in the time of life such as new birth and the return of growth versus January's winter which is the time of the dead.*

*Marriage was consummated, followed by a wedding feast or harvest also referred to as the* **feast of the tabernacle**, *which takes place in the seventh month (September).* This is similar to **Kwanzaa which is an attempt to replicate the West African Israelite feast of the harvest; however harvest is not in the winter, thus to celebrate the harvest on December 26$^{th}$ through January 1$^{st}$ is a mockery. Women covered their heads**, *abstaining from unclean foods (i.e. pork, crabs, lobsters, and shrimp). Heterosexuality was law and culture. The patriarchal society was the point of stability with a ruling King and belief in the black Messiah.*

West African Israelite religion was classified as Islamic as early as the 1200s. Israelites differ from Arabs Muslims and Semitic Ishmaelites. However, numerous Israelites living in West Africa converted to Islam. For example, *Mansa Musa (1280-1337A.D.) was an Israelite who converted to Islam.* The sons of Ishmael and other Arabs Muslims played a sinister role as prolific and disturbingly innovative slave traders who sold the Israelites to the European Christian sons of Japheth. Israelites like Mansa Musa continued to forsake their **Covenant of the Ten Commandments "Thou shalt not serve any gods besides me."** *(Exodus 20:3)* converting and serving other gods, the Israelites failed God. They received baptism into the "religion of slavery" in the Americas and fulfilled the Biblical prophecy of serving gods of wood and stone. ***Deuteronomy 28: 36** "The LORD SHALL BRING THEE, AND THY KING WHICH THOU SHALT SET OVER THEE, UNTO A NATION WHICH NEITHER THOU NOR THY FATHERS HAVE KNOWN; AND THERE SHALT THOU **serve other gods, wood and stone."** (E.g. the **wood is** symbolic for the **Christian Cross** and the **stone is** symbolic for **Islam's Kaaba**).*

When the slaves were baptized into the "religion of slavery", they eradicated their West African Israelite religious identity and discarded in order to be loyal subservient American and European-minded Christians. The mystery of the Bible is forever mysterious due to the fact that the American Christian sons of Japheth used the Israelites Bible to so-called enslave the Israelites. However, the power of the Bible used the American Christian Gentile sons of Japheth to fulfill the Biblical codification of the supreme rule of law, therefore being Baptize into the religion of slavery would be the method of how the Israelites would fulfill Biblical prophecy *(Deuteronomy 28:47-48)* in the Americas.

The so-called American, Christian sons of Japheth placed a white face *(i.e. Elvis Presley)* on the Black man's Rock and Roll and a white face on a Black Moses in the *Ten Commandments* (1956). The American Christians placed a white face on the Biblical Black Jesus and reclassified the Bible as a Christian book. For example, the white image ***of Cesare Borgia Jesus (1475-1507)*** was indoctrinated into the minds and hearts of the Hebrew children of slavery.

## ELDER MARK MAKABI

The image of the Paleface Jesus was a construct of Pope <u>Clement VII</u> and Pope Paul III who were afraid that the original images of Biblical figures (people of color) would lead to so-called whites following those people who favored the images of Christ (Israelites). The advancing caliphates and empires of the Muslim world ruled parts of Eastern and Southern Europe all with areas of North and West Africa, and of course, the Arabian Peninsula stretch out over Central to Southeast Asia.

As the Sistine Chapel fresco of *The Last Supper* (1541) was being completed, Pope Paul III instructed Michelangelo to depict Biblical figures as white, based on members of his family and papal figures such as the ruthless Cesare Borgia (1475-1507), illegitimate son of pope Alexander VI. Using images of whites and the Israelite acceptance of this is what led to the legitimacy of slavery according to the European sons of Japheth. This is why Israelites downfall into slavery in Europe and the Americas was rooted in the sin of accepting a Paleface image of a Black God; idolatry is completely wrong.

True images of the Black Jesus or reference to the truth have been seen in numerous Hollywood films and TV shows along with original images in religious art and literature from the beginning of Christianity in Europe. A number of programs have established a clearer understanding that Jesus, was a Black man as all Israelites were and continue to be. These programs include but are not limited to *Good Times (1974) "Black Jesus" episode; from Shaka Zulu (1986), the European invader states the slaves are the "Wandering Jews"; in Amistad (1997), a slave is wearing a "Star of David" on the slave ship. In Roots (1977) it is revealed that the slaves from West Africa spoke the Hebrew (Aramaic) language; in "Green Pas-*

ture Movie" (1936), Bruce Almighty (2003) God is a Black man, and Lucifer (2016 Fox TV-series) the Devil is a white man.* The American Christian captors were clever in selecting Biblical scriptures referring to slavery when reading from the Bible to the slaves, similar to **the scene from 12 Years a Slave movie (2013). This is a clear statement when considering the fact**, it was against the laws of America for the Israelite captives to learn to read or write their abstract English language, so they would never know Jesus the Christ and other Israelites had "hair of wool and skin of bronze burnt in an oven " (Revelations 1:14-15).

Among the verses used to justify and rationalize slavery in the minds of the American, Christian captors was **Colossians 3:22.** It is one of the popular verses the American Christian oppressors read to the slaves following baptism into the religion of slavery. **"Servants, obey in all things your masters according to the flesh**; **not with eyeservice, as menpleasers; but in singleness of heart, fearing God.**" However, what the American Christians oppressors did not understand about these scriptures is that Paul wrote in the letter addressed Israelite brotherhood (**Colossian's 1:2 is written to the SAINTS, living saints who led the new "Christian" Israelite-based religion challenged by Roman and Greek paganism and persecution**) **The saints are Israelites (Psalm 148:14).** With this in mind, Colossians 3:22 refers to the law of the Torah (First Testament) on how an Israelite employer (master) should treat an Israelite employee (servant - *Leviticus 25:39-40*). This explains *Colossians 4:1)* "*Masters, give unto your servants that which is just and equal; knowing that ye also have a Master in Heaven*" which is a testimony against the American Christians captors unjust treatment of the Hebrew slaves.

## Elder Mark Makabi

In Harrisburg, Pennsylvania (2012), an atheist organization (Pennsylvania Nonbelievers, Inc.) placed a billboard ad featuring an image of a black man with a yoke around his neck *(Deuteronomy 28:48)* and the scriptures from **Colossians 3:22 "Slave Obey Your Masters"** with the alleged intent to place many similar billboards throughout America. Therefore, I wrote a letter, *"Israelites Responds to Atheist"*, to this American atheist organization to educate and supported them in erecting similar billboard ads throughout America. For their cause supported and illuminated the remembrances of our Israelite (Biblical) holocaust of slavery in the Americas.

The American Christian miseducation of the **Curse of Ham** taught that people of color, including the Israelites deserved to be slaves. The curse of dark skin (high pigmentation) was supposedly removed through the baptism. The curse of Ham was used to baptize the West African Israelites into the religion of slavery. However, what the American Christian sons of Japheth did not comprehend was that **Canaan** was cursed not Ham. The children of slavery are from the lineage of Shem *(a Semitic race)* and not Hamitic or Africans. The sons of Noah, Shem, Ham, and Japheth were Black *(Shem settled in Asia, Ham in Africa, and Japheth in the Caucasus Mountains).* The curse of Canaan had nothing to do with pigmentation **(but the first born son)** as many American racist sons of Japheth believed and continue to act upon. However, the curse that is related to color of pigmentation is called **leprosy,** *"white as snow"*, **Numbers 12:10**. *Therefore, the children of slavery are under the* **Curse of Disobedience** *and the Canaanites (an African nation) were/are under the* **Curse of Canaan.** *The Israelites and Canaanites have black pigmentation; however, one is Semitic and* *the other Hamitic.* In addition, when the enslaved men and women came to the Americas in slave ships they were not allowed to read, write, or speak their Hebrew language, or continue to practice their West African Israelite religion.

Since the American Christian sons of Japheth prospered as the masters over the Hebrew-Israelite slaves, many slaves became baptized into the religion of slavery. Slaves entered the religion with the hope of achieving the same prosperity, liberty, life of luxury, and equality. However, in the process of being Christian slaves, many lost their religious identity over a period of 300 years. Nevertheless, the **power of the Negro Spirituals** preserved the religious Israelite identity among the children of slavery in a musical form. This musical phone had a number of religion references that were coded, enabling the Israelite slaves to outwit the American Gentile sons of Japheth. Many of the descendants of slaves in the Americas do not seem to understand this miraculous preservation of their *Israelite (Biblical) heritage,* which maybe a byproduct of them being baptized in the religion of slavery in the Americas.

The religious philosophies of the ***sons of Esau (Edomites), "Judaism, "the sons of Ishmael, "Islam," and the European Gentile sons of Japheth "Christianity"*** *plagiarized, incorporated, and corrupted many aspects of the Biblical religion, culture, and principles of the Israelites.* The God of Abraham, Isaac, and Jacob did not ordain any nation to his priesthood and servants except the Israelites. **Psalms 147:19-20 (NIV)** "He has revealed his **word to JACOB**, his laws and decrees to **ISRAEL. He has done this for no other nation; they do not know his laws. Praise the** Lord." Nevertheless, The Israelites *(descendant of slaves)* were chosen to be servants of the Most High, and once they refused to serve their God of Israel, they were cursed with serving their enemies for 400 years as bondmen and bondwomen in America *(New Egypt, Babylon, and Sodom and Gomorrah)*.

## BLACKS

**The Color of Race:** Pigmentation does not determine your race; thus, from the warp minded of a *Swedish named Carl Linnaeus (1717-1778)* and a *German named Johann Friedrich Blumenbach (1752-1840),* the division of humanity into five races, based on skin color, arose. The races were and continue to be defined as *White, Yellow, Brown, Black, and Red*. Race became a standard similar to the caste system of India by which a person was defined and valued: the lighter the better, the darker the worst within all races of color. This was unfortunately adopted by many of the descendants of slaves in the Americas as their standard of racial classification. **Moreover, nations with similar skin colors are not of the same race, ethnicity, nation, or culture.**

**Geography**: In reference to race it is a mystical land of the color hue.

**Demographics**: An estimate of over 25 million Israelites in America.

*Clarifying the blur national, racial, and color lines:* The so-called Blacks were transported in slave ships from West Africa to the Americas. Africa is a continent which has fifty-three (53) countries and was most likely named after a Phoenician prefix (Afar) and Latin suffix (ica), speaking various European Languages, and classifying their national and racial identity as a color.

**Race:** The division of humanity based on ***language,*** *land,* ***fam-***

# BYWORD

*ilies (ethnicities), cultures, or nations;* moreover, the seed of the father determine the racial and national heritage of a child, accept when one has *an Israelite mother married to a foreigner*.

### GENESIS 10, The Sons of Noah

- **Shem, (Asia)** father of the Semitic race: Sumerians, Assyrians, Chaldeans, Hebrews, Israelites etc. The Asians of antiquity were people of color.
- **Ham, (Africa) father of** the Hamitic race: Phoenicians (Sidon) Egyptians or Khem, Africans, Ethiopians or Cush, Nubians, Canaanites, Hittites etc.
- **Japheth (Caucasus Mountains)**, father of the Japhetic race: Europeans such as Caucasians, Spanish, Portuguese, French, Irish, Dutch, Greeks, Romans, British, Germans, Slavs, Russians, Native American Indians etc.
- Shem, Japheth, and Ham were brothers and black men.

**Black**: is a color pertaining to pigmentation. Negros are not of Ham or Hamites.

**Esau (Edomites):** Esau came out **HAIRY & RED** pertaining to his pigmentation *(i.e. relating to the term **RED-NECK)**.* The modern-day Israelis. (i.e. Benjamin Netanyahu etc.)

**Albinos:** The Gentile Caucasians are Albinos.

**Albinism Scientific Perspective:** A genetic mutation that influences the creation of melanin. The cell melanocyte controls the production of hair, skin, and eye pigmentation; although the melanocytes are existing, genetic mutation interrupts their production to allocate to their keratinocytes cells.

**Health Benefits of Melanin of Darker Black Skin:** Protects skin from the sun damage, younger looking-skin, and targets free-radicals.

*"I AM BLACK, BUT COMELY,"* from King Solomon (Songs of Solomon 1:5).

**Who's Your Father?** Who named Israelite's Blacks?

**In regards to your national identity,** Black is Beautiful however it's not a nationality.

**Byword guides us back to our nation:**
>Biblical nation of Israel
>Race: Semitic
>Color of skin: Seven shades of brown
>Language: Hebrew
>Motherland: Jerusalem, Israel

## AFRO-BRAZILIANS

**Historical Highlight:** The Israelite holocaust of slavery in Brazil first began in Africa where the Ishmaelite Arab Muslims sold Israelites to Christians Europeans. Moreover, it is estimated that 89% of the Israelites survived the holocaust of the middle passage, and over 12 million were imported to the Americas and 4.86 million to Brazil. The business of slave trading was prosperous, and the Israelite captives built the infrastructure and economic wealth of Brazil. Slavery was abolished on May 3 1888 however racism continues in Brazil. We remember the ***great Israelite General Zumbi dos Palmares, our Grand Capoiera,*** *Edson **"Pele"** Arantes do Nascimento,* ***and many others.***

**Origin of the name:** The origin of the name seems to be a mystery; however, the most consistent version is that Brazil was named after the "Brazilwood tree" by the Portuguese with the root words **"Pau-Brasil" (redwood tree).** The reddish wood resembled represented red hot embers and was an excellent source of red dye.

**Geography**: South America.

**Demographics**: An estimate of 44.7% of the population are Israelites *(descendants of slaves).*

*Clarifying the blur national, racial, and color lines:* *The so-called Afro-Brazilians were transported in slave ships from West Africa to the Americas. Africa is a continent which has fifty-three (53) countries and was most likely named after a Phoenician prefix and Latin suffix, speaking Portuguese, and classifying their national and racial identity after the name of the land that most likely the Portuguese renamed as "[Land of] Redwood Trees".*

**Afro**: An abbreviation for African or referring to a 1960s and '70s hairstyle celebrating Israelite pride, power, dignity, and glory.

**Brazil**: Portuguese Pau and Brasil for the Redwood Tree.

**Brazilian Minstrels**: Brazil produces a racist minstrel image **"Adelaide"**

**Who's Your Father?** Who named Israelite's Afro-Brazilians?

**In regards to your national identity, Afro-Brazilians is a byword:** - Ridicule

**Byword guides us back to our nation:**
    Biblical nation of Israel
    Race: Semitic
    Pigmentation: Seven shades of blackness
    Language: Hebrew
    Homeland: Jerusalem, Israel

## MULATTO

**Origin of the name**: The name seems too derived from the Portuguese and/or Spanish for mix breed meaning "mule". However, the term denotes a person with one so-called Black parent and one so-called White parent. In many cultures, including American culture the term is derogatory.

**Geography**: the Americas.

**Demographics**: An estimate of individuals who identify as Mulattos in the Americas is not known.

*Clarifying the blur national, racial, and color lines: The so-called Mulattos were transported in slave ships from West Africa to the Americas. Africa is a continent which has fifty-three (53) countries and was most likely named after a Phoenician prefix and Latin suffix, speaking various European languages, and classifying their national and racial identity, based on the racial classification of skin color by the warp minds of the European Gentile sons of Japheth.*

**Mulatto:** Offspring of so-called Black and White parents.

**One Drop Rules! Negro Blood** Historically, it was custom for most Mulattos to deny their Negro blood in order to improve their social and economic status in the Americas among the European Gentile sons of Japheth. Moreover, the European Gentile sons of Japheth understood that one drop of the Negro blood was superior, and thus dominant; therefore they classified and continue to classify a person with one drop as a Negro or Black. Nevertheless, in the near feature, it will be very popular or expedient for many nations to start claiming that they have one drop of Negro blood.

**Ezekiel 47:22-23** "And it shall come to pass, that ye shall divide it by lot for an inheritance unto you (referring to Israelites), and to **the strangers that sojourn among you,** which **shall beget children among you**: and they shall be unto you as born in the country among the **Children of Israel;** they shall have inheritance with you among the tribes of Israel."

**Who's Your Father?** Who named Israelite's Mulattos?

**In regards to your national identity, Mulatto is a byword:**

- Mockery

**Byword guides us back to our nation:**

    Biblical nation of Israel

    Race: Semitic

    Color of skin: Seven shades of brown

    Language: Hebrew

    Motherland: Jerusalem, Israel

## AFRO BLACK CANADIANS

**Historical Highlight:** Canada has been considered a sanctuary for the fugitive Israelite slaves; however slavery did exist from 1600-1800. There was a substantial Israelite settlement in Nova Scotia that followed the British exodus from New York in 1783, the end of the American Revolution. In addition, Israelites fled to Canada after the Fugitive Slave Act (1851) following the Compromise of 1850 which established the Mason-Dixon Line, and further marginalized Israelites in American society with significantly defined slave states and free states. However, with the Fugitive Slave Act, even free Israelite men, women, and children could be seized and returned to slavery. In addition the Compromise 1850, allowed slave states to use their slave population as means to establish political blocks in the House of Representatives. The law stated that the

Israelite man or woman was 3/5ths human according to the American Gentile sons of Japheth. This was a complete mockery of our humanity, greatness, and ingenuity.

Lieutenant Governor John Colborne of Canada granted Israelites sanctuary. The Honorable **Josiah Henson** was a great Israelite who established the *Dawn Institute and the city of Dresden, Ontario. Dresden, Ontario* was a model community established in Canada with a mission to educate self-emancipated Israelites (runaway slaves) and help them adjust to life in a free and relatively equal society. Josiah Henson contributed to the writing of the best-seller book of its time *Uncle Tom's Cabin* which influenced the commencement of the American Civil War. The truth is Uncle Tom was no "Tom"; he was an Israelite hero for freedom.

**Origin of the name** the name Canada is derived from the natives Iroquoian word *Kanata,* which means "village." **Geography**: North America.

**Demographics**: An estimate of 2.7% of the population are Israelites *(the descendants of slaves).*

*Clarifying the blur national, racial, and color lines:* The so-called Afro-Black Canadians were transported in slave ships from West Africa to the Americas. Africa is a continent which has fifty-three (53) countries and was most likely named after a Phoenician prefix (Afar) and Latin suffix (ica), speaking English or French, and classifying their national and racial identity from a word that derives from the Iroquois word for "village".

**Canada:** village

**Who's Your Father?** Who named Israelite's Afro-Black Canadians?

# BYWORD

**In regards to your national identity, Afro-Canadian is a byword:** - Ridicule

**Byword guides us back to our nation:**
    Biblical nation of Israel
    Race: Semitic
    Pigmentation: Seven shades of blackness
    Language: Hebrew
    Homeland: Jerusalem, Israel

## AFRO-PERUVIANS

**Historical Highlight:** Peru is where the Inca Empire had been established from the 13th to the 16th centuries. In 1512, Israelite captives arrived with the Spanish conquistadors as soldiers and skilled tradesmen. They performed skilled functions such as manufacturing swords, lances, and rosaries for the Spanish army. The Israelite activity contributed to the overall economic and social development of Peru. Approximately 95,000 Israelites captives were brought to Peru during the South American Slave Trade. Slave revolts occurred until slavery was abolished in 1854.

In November 2009, the government of Peru issued an official apology to Israelites *(Afro-Peruvians)* for 400 years of racial injustice. Moreover, there was a public ceremony on *December 7, 2009* with the presence of President Garcia which acknowledged Peru's crimes against the Israelites.

**Origin of the name**: The origin and meaning of Peru is obscure; the popular theory is it derives from the native word "biru" meaning "river" or it is a name of an Indian Chieftain "Beru".

**Geography**: South America.

**Demographics**: An estimate of 1.5-10% of the population are Israelites *(descendants of slaves)*.

***Clarifying the blur national, racial, and color lines***: *The so-called Afro-Peruvians were transported in slave ships from West Africa to the Americas. Africa is a continent which has fifty-three (53) countries and was most likely named after a Phoenician prefix (Afar) and Latin suffix (ica), speaking Spanish, and classifying their national and racial identity from an Inca word meaning river or the name of a famous chieftain.*

**Peru:** Name of an Indian Chieftain "Beru" or "river".

**Peruvian Minstrels:** Peru produces a racist show **"El Negro Mama"**

**Who's Your Father?** Who named Israelite's Afro-Peruvians?

**In regards to your national identity, Afro-Peruvian is a by-word:** - Mockery

**Byword guides us back to our nation:**

    Biblical nation of Israel
    Race: Semitic
    Color of skin: Seven shades of brown
    Language: Hebrew
    Motherland: Jerusalem, Israel

## PANAMANIANS

**Historical Highlight:** The history of slavery in Panama is extensive. The Spanish imported Israelites captives in the 16th century. Diego de Nicosia brought Israelite slaves to a region now called "***Nombre De Dios***". The earliest document of slaves in Panama was 1509. Division among Israelites in the region between

## BYWORD

Mesoamerica and the Caribbean has been evident for centuries. One example of the division was between the West Indians and Panamanians. The West Indians worked for the United Fruit Company (1899-1984, which is now The Chiquita Brands International) believed the Panamanians were Latinized (similar to the Dominicans of the Republic). Panamanians viewed the West Indians as tokens for the Americans who had facilitated the takeover and division of Panama for the United States of America (e.g. the Panama Canal). Did the West Indians and Panamanians know or understand that they were and remain a divided nation of the Biblical nation of Israel?

**Origin of the name**: Derives from the Cueva Indian language meaning "place of abundance of fish" or "place of many fish".

**Geography**: Central America.

**Demographics**: An estimate of 14% of the population are Israelites *(descendants of slaves)*.

***Clarifying the blur national, racial, and color lines****: The so-called Panamanians were transported in slave ships from West Africa to the Americas. Africa is a continent which has fifty-three (53) countries and was most likely named after a Phoenician prefix and Latin suffix, speaking Spanish and English, and classifying their national and racial identity after the land the Cueva Indian word for "place of abundance of fish" or "place of many fish".*

**Panama:** "abundance of fish"

**Who's Your Father?** Who named Israelite's Panamanians?

**In regards to your national identity, Panamanian is a byword:** -Ridicule

**Byword guides us back to our nation:**

## Elder Mark Makabi

Biblical nation of Israel
Race: Semitic
Pigmentation: Seven shades of brown
Language: Hebrew
Homeland: Jerusalem, Israel

### AFRO-FRENCH GUIANESE

**Historical Highlight:** In 1604, the French established Guiana as a colonial possession. Israelite slaves were imported to finance the French sugar cane and coffee industries. French Guiana was known for its revolts, maroons, and **Motier de La Fayette** (1757-1834). Lafayette was an American Revolutionary War hero and international abolitionist. His vision of a liberated Israelite people within world society, primarily American; however, considering the times, LaFayette decided to begin his social experiment with emancipation in Cayenne, French Guiana. He sought to purchase land for freed Israelites captives to settle.

The emancipation of the Israelite captives occurred on May 21, 1838. On May 21, 2001, the French government enacted the ***"Taubira Law"***; this law recognized the Israelite holocaust of slavery as "crimes against humanity."

**Origin of the name**: The name was given by the French which is a form of an Amerindian and/or Caribbean word which means "land of many waters"

**Geography**: South America.

**Demographics**: An estimate of 66% of the population are Israelites *(the descendants of slaves)*.

*Clarifying the blur national, racial, and color lines: The so-called Afro-French Guianese were transported in slave ships*

## BYWORD

*from West Africa to the Americas. Africa is a continent which has fifty-three (53) countries and was most likely named after a Phoenician prefix and Latin suffix, speaking French and Creole languages, classifying their national and racial identity from the racial classification from a European nation, and an Amerindian and/or Caribbean word which means "land of many waters".*

**French Guianese:** "land of waters" or "French land of waters"

**Who's Your Father?** Who named Israelite's Afro-French Guianese?

**In regards to your national identity, Afro-Guianese is a byword:** - Mockery

**Byword guides us back to our nation:**
    Biblical nation of Israel
    Race: Semitic
    Color of skin: Seven shades of brown
    Language: Hebrew
    Motherland: Jerusalem, Israel

## MARTINICANS

**Historical Highlight:** Martinique is a story of colonization, slavery, plantations, and oppression. The French arrived in 1635 and encountered the native Kalipunas *(so-called Caribs)*. By 1680, 80% of the population were Israelites slaves, 12% Europeans, with 8% mixed and/or Kalipunas Amerindian descent. With the Israelites in the majority, how the feeble European Gentile sons Japheth ruled the mighty Biblical nation of Israel with ease remains shocking. In 1636, King Louis III sanctioned the introduction of French slavery in the Caribbean. Slavery was abolished on May 22, 1848. In addition, the long-term continuity of the plantation economy and assimilation of the Israelites into the French culture was and remains an example of one of the horrific effects of the holocaust of slavery in the Americas. Nevertheless, the process of assimilation is to develop an artificial high standard of living based on a caste system centered on ancestry. It was this warped philosophy that kept the slaves under French control. Martinique is currently not a sovereign nation but remains a French territory.

**Origin of the name**: The original name could have been "Madinina", which means "the island of flowers" or "Mantinino", "island of women" in the Arawak language. In 1493, Christopher Columbus viewed but never landed on the island, yet he renamed it "Martinica" in honor of a Spanish man named Martin (Martinique).

**Geography**: Caribbean.

**Demographics**: An estimate of 90% of the population are Israelites *(descendant of slaves)*.

*Clarifying the blur national, racial, and color lines*: *The so-called Martinicans were transported in slave ships from West Africa to the Americas. Africa is a continent which has fifty-three (53) countries and was most likely named after a Phoenician prefix (Afar) and Latin suffix (ica), speaking French, and classifying their national and racial identity after the name of the island that an Italian named after a Spanish man.*

**Martinique:** Name after Martin who the European Gentiles presumptuously called saint.

**Who's Your Father?** Who named Israelite's Martinicans?

**In regards to your national identity, Martinican is a byword** - Ridicule

# BYWORD

**Byword guides us back to our nation:**
    Biblical nation of Israel
    Race: Semitic
    Pigmentation: Seven shades of blackness
    Language: Hebrew
    Homeland: Jerusalem, Israel

## AFRO-PARAGUAYANS

**Historical Highlight:** Racism, immense poverty, racial discrimination, exclusion from political participation, and violent displacement by the Paraguayan state is the story of the Israelite Biblical holocaust of slavery and modern racism in Paraguay. In addition, the invisible Israelite slaves were known as *"pardos"* (or "brown ones" a pejorative like the word "nigger") during the colonial era. By 1785, Israelite slaves in captivity represented 11% of the population; after Paraguay's independence in 1812, many Israelites were forced back into slavery. However, in 1842 Paraguay government declared the "law of the free womb "which stated that the "children of slaves born after that date will be free on their 24$^{th}$ birthday; this was a sociological twist on an evil political and cultural institution (slavery). By 1869, slavery was completely abolished.

**Origin of the name**: The most popular historical opinion is that the name derives from the river that divides east from the west of the nation. There are several historical sources of the meaning such as "water of Paraguay, "or in the Tupi-Guarani language, "para" (river), "Gua" (Crown), meaning "crowned river."

**Geography**: South America.

**Demographics**: An estimate of 0.1% of the population are Israelites *(the descendants of slaves)*

***Clarifying the blur national, racial, and color lines****: The so-called Afro-Paraguayans were transported in slave ships from West Africa to the Americas. Africa is a continent which has fifty-three (53) countries and was most likely named after a Phoenician prefix (Afar) and Latin suffix (ica), speaking Spanish, and classifying their national and racial identity based on a word in the Tupi-Guarani language that means "crowned river" or "the royal river".*

**Paraguay**: From the Tupi-Guarani language "Crown river"

**Who's Your Father?** Who named Israelite's Afro-Paraguayans?

**In regards to your national identity, Afro-Paraguayan is a byword:** - Mockery

**Byword guides us back to our nation:**

    Biblical nation of Israel

    Race: Semitic

    Color of skin: Seven shades of brown

    Language: Hebrew

    Motherland: Jerusalem, Israel

## CAYMANIANS

**Historical Highlight:** The Cayman Islands were magnets for ruthless pirates such as *"Sir Henry Morgan"* and *"Black Beard."* "One of the most famous shipwrecks was *"The Wreck of the Ten Tails" (1794).* Within the Caymans, **Pedro St. James Castle** remains. Originally the "Castle" was a home of a plantation owner, William Eden, who sold cotton and mahogany. This historic site was built by the Israelite captives. In some accounts the Caymans have been dubbed the *"Birthplace of Democracy"* within the Cayman Islands. It was at the "Catle" on May 3, 1835, that Robert Thompson, at the request of Governor Howe Peter Browne, the Second Marquess of Sligo (Sligo, Ireland) proclaimed the abolition of slavery on Grand Cayman. 950 Israelites captives were owned by 116 families on Grand Cayman. The Cayman Islands are a British territory.

**Origin of the name:** Columbus named the island "Las Tortugas" (Turtles) because of the abundance of turtles. However, Cayman derives from Kalipuna word for "marine alligators" (caiman) found on the island.

**Geography**: Caribbean.

**Demographics**: An estimate of 60% of the population are Israelites *(descendants of slaves)*

***Clarifying the blur national, racial, and color lines***: *The so-called Caymanians were transported in slave ships from West Africa to the Americas. Africa is a continent which has fifty-three (53) countries and was most likely named after a Phoenician prefix and Latin suffix, speaking the English, and classifying their national and racial identity after the name of the island which derives from a word in the Kalipuna language meaning "alligator" or "marine alligator". The Kalipunas were identified as Caribs by the Spanish Gentile sons of Japheth.*

**Cayman island:** "Marine Alligators"

**Who's Your Father?** Who named Israelite's Caymanians?

**In regards to your national identity, Caymanian is a byword:** - Ridicule

**Byword guides us back to our nation:**
    Biblical nation of Israel
    Race: Semitic

## ELDER MARK MAKABI

Pigmentation: Seven shades of blackness
Language: Hebrew
Homeland: Jerusalem, Israel

### BITTER HERBS!

*Blow the trumpets in the new moon,*
*Sing in the spring time for life's song,*
*Swing into spring, let's celebrate,*
*Spring in the New Year, let's cultivate,*
*Remember the past over the pass,*
*Remember to pass over the task,*
**And eat those bitter herbs,**
*Own the confession,*
*Circumcise the heart,*
*Taste the affliction,*
*Past to pass,*
*Prepare the unleavened bread,*
*Water the soul,*
*Lamb the meat,*
*Pray to the east,*
**And drink those bitter herbs,**
*Slaves, own your cotton,*
*Slaves, own your terms of endearment,*
*Slaves, own your jazz, hip-hop, rock and roll,*
*Slaves, own your calypso, reggae, gospel and your soul,*
*Slaves own your captivity,*
*Slaves, own your Biblical identity,*
**And eat those bitter herbs,**
*Sodom and Gomorrah, own your fire,*
*Egypt, own your plagues,*

# BYWORD

*Babylon, own the handwriting wall,*
*Rome, own your burning fall,*
*America, own your racist reprisal,*
*Israelites, own your Bible,*
*Ishmael, own your fatal seal for your slave trading zeal,*
*Edom, own your hell Obadiah revealed,*
***And drink those bitter herbs,***
*Goldenseal, wormwood, horehound, and yarrow,*
*Cleanliness ensues the straight and narrow,*
*Own the confession,*
*Circumcise the heart,*
*Taste the affliction,*
*Past to pass,*
*Prepare the unleavened bread,*
*Lamb the meat,*
*Pray to the east,*
***And eat those bitter herbs…***

# CHAPTER 4
# SLAVE CODES FOR BLACK CODES

## "The Biblical Codification for the Supreme Rule of Law"

The Israelites were and remain innovators of science, politics, natural and moral law, agriculture, culture, education, medicine, morality, humanity, finance, engineering, creative arts, music, philosophy, and true religion. The carnal minds of the European Gentile sons of Japheth developed the concept, the world was flat from the Moors (i.e. Israelite's *e.g.* **Revelation 7:1** *"And after these things I saw four angels standing on the **FOUR CORNERS** of the **EARTH**, ... "*) however, the Israelites had advanced scientific knowledge that predates the Gentile sons of Japheth by thousands of years, notably with the concept that the world was flat with a spherical circumference. "He sits enthroned above the *circle* of the earth, and its people are like grasshoppers. He stretches out the heavens like a canopy, and spreads them out like a tent to live in" (Isaiah 40:22). Circa 1876 B.C. our founding Hebrew fathers Abraham, Isaac, and Jacob of the Biblical nation of Israel established a righteous model for all Israelites to emulate in the formation of their patriarchal society ruled

# BYWORD

by Israelite Kings *(i.e. **King David, King Solomon, King Hezekiah, King Josiah, and the reigning King of kings and Lord of lords the Israelite Messiah Jesus the Christ**).* The Covenant exclusively established with Abraham, Isaac, Jacob, and the 12 tribes of Israel fortified the Kingdom of Israel which is the Kingdom of Heaven on Earth. The Kingdom of Heaven on Earth is a physical, spiritual, political, cultural, and commercial epicenter representative of God's plan as to how all people of Earth should live. **Our Israelite covenant is our everlasting legal binding constitution that was sealed in blood, written in stone** *(e.g. circumcision, sacrificial Lamb, and the Ten Commandments)*, **and founded on the principles of righteousness that established the government of the Biblical nation of Israel as a sovereign, theocratic nation ruled by a monarch with the favor of the God of Israel.**

The children of Israel were instructed by God to rule their theocratic nation according to their Biblical laws in righteousness. They exercised their freedom of choice to agree to the terms of receiving the blessings for their obedience or the curses for their disobedience. However, the misuse of their freewill and their stiff-necked resistance led to their downfall. They constantly rebelled, pursuing the adoption of other cultures and spirituality among nations such as *Assyrians, Egyptians, Cushites, Persians, Babylonians, Canaanites, Romans, Greeks, etc. This resulted in occupations, expulsions, slavery, and domination by Egyptians, Assyrians, Persians, Babylonians, Greeks, Romans, and centuries later the European and American sons of Japheth.* It was the fall of the Biblical nation of Israel that led them to flee from the Promise Land from the persecution of the Romans (70-135 A.D.) to take refuge in the land of Ham in *West*

*Africa.* Later, the Israelites came on slave ships via middle passage into the Americas as prophesized by the Israelite prophet Moses.

**DEUTERONOMY 28:68 King James Version** "And the LORD shall bring thee into **Egypt again with SHIPS**, by the way whereof I spake unto thee, Thou shalt see it no more again: and there ye shall be **sold** unto your **enemies** for **bondmen and bondwomen,** and no man shall buy you." Thus, "Egypt again" *symbolizes America as the new Egypt and the house of bondage.* **EXODUS 20:1-2** "And God spake all these words, saying, I am the LORD thy God, which have brought thee out of the land of Egypt, out of **the HOUSE of BONDAGE.** "Thus, the enslaved Biblical nation of Israel would be removed from their theocratic, sovereign state and thrust into an alien and strange sociopolitical system that claimed to be a democracy governed on a theory of equality while practicing a perverse brand of capitalism that was enforced by a totalitarian system rooted in the American legal institution of the slave codes and black codes.

The slave codes and black codes proved that Christian America's so-called democracy of equality was never equal and would set forth the governance of two separate nations that would be governed under two separate rule of laws for the American Gentile sons of Japheth and the Hebrew sons of Jacob. The slave codes were inhumane laws that were practiced under the American totalitarianism political system; these slave codes exclusively targeted the Israelite captives to establish social controls, the master-slave order, servile behaviors (psychological bondage), and define the status of the slaves as property to dehumanize the Israelite captives in the American colonies and later the nation.

## BYWORD

The European and later American sons of Japheth had traveled thousands of miles during the middle passage to invade the West African Israelite place of refuge and then these heathens made it a crime for the Israelite captives to travel without a written permission from their oppressors even if they were free under the slave codes (*i.e. licenses such as manumission papers for the free and letters of passage for slaves*). However, the sons of Ishmael, the sons of Esau and the American sons of Japheth pillaged humans, gold, minerals, and land to claim ownership and then these criminals made it a crime for the Israelite captives to own property or even their own name under the slave codes. The American Christian sons of Japheth could congregate to worship their Sun god on Sunday; however, these American Christian thugs made it a crime for the Israelite captives to congregate with their brother and sisters without a Caucasian present under the slave codes and later black codes. (i.e. Nate Parker – Classic Movie Birth of a Nation 2016)

America's immoral predisposition formulated with the establishment of murdering the natives of the Americas, stealing their lands, and the formation of the slave codes and black codes which made America powerful, wealthy, and provided privileges for the sons of Esau (***Revelation 2:9*** – *The impostor Jews are a combination of three separate nations the Edomites, Europeans that descended from Russia ( Khazars), and Germany (Ashkenazi) versus the Hebrew children of Israel),* and the American Gentile sons of Japheth. However, the formation of the slave codes was a sinister investment by a few exclusive Caucasian men to divide and conquer across the color lines and maintain their power, wealth, and control. This plot began when poor, indentured Israelites and Caucasian servants united under Nathaniel Bacon (during the Bacon's rebellion, 1675-1676) against the Governor of Virginia, William Berkeley. The colonists were being attacked by Native American tribes, and the governor did little to assist in the battles. The rebellion was a classist uprising with the poor against the rich. However, the sentiment toward people of color originally focused on Native American tribes soon shifted to Israelite indentured servants and gave the racists among the Virginians justification for separation of the races and the rationalization of generational indentured servitude which evolved into slave codes and definition of race per individual based on the mother's origin. Many Israelite women bore children for Caucasian men through rape and coercion, and their children remained in slavery for another 189 years.

America's capitalism prospered under a totalitarian government predicated on a theory of democracy while utilizing terrorism (i.e. the Compromise of 1850, The Fugitive Slave Act of 1850, and support of the KKK in 1866) to enforce the slave codes and later black codes. Nevertheless, the slaves codes laid the legal foundation that spearheaded the anti-Semitic institution of racism in the Americas which redefined and Hellenized the Biblical nation of Israel spiritually, culturally, socially, religiously, politically, racially, and nationally. Therefore, it would be through the American political and legal system that the European colonists and their white indentured servants would use to separate themselves from the Israelite captives to violate their human righteousness and commence the greatest horrific crimes against humanity characterized as the ***Israelite (Biblical) holocaust of slavery in the Americas.***

In 1865, the American Civil War ended; however, the defeated

Confederate states moved quickly to ratify the black codes to maintain their delusional, so-called white supremacy ideology, social controls over the emancipated slaves (freedmen) and freeman (free before the war), and to illegally supersede the American Emancipation Proclamation, as well as the U.S. Constitution's ***Thirteenth Amendment*** which *abolished slavery,* the ***Fourteenth Amendment*** *which granted state and federal citizenship for the emancipated slaves,* and the ***Fifteenth Amendment*** *which prohibited the federal and state governments from denying a U.S. citizen the right to vote based on their color and/or race.*

The black codes can be characterized as anti-Semitic racist laws that legitimized barbaric crimes by heathens who criminalized their victims under a totalitarian political system which was supported by the laws of the American legal and political institution. For example, the American Gentile sons of Japheth orchestrated the enslavement of the Israelites by Arabs slave traders (few Europeans ever did their own proverbial dirty work in Africa). Then these thugs made it a crime for any Israelite captive to raise insurrections for their freedom; *however, movies such as Spartacus glorified insurrection against Rome while Israelites remain in psychological bondage to this day in the New Rome of the United States.* Insurrection which was punishable by death under the slave codes. Later, these same criminals, Caucasian sons of Japheth made it a crime for the Israelite citizens not slaves of the United States to bear arms or exercise their human, civil, and legal rights to self-defense under the black codes from as early as 1866 to as late as the 1970s throughout the United States due to the lack of enforcement of the Civil Rights Act of 1964 and Voting Rights Act of 1965.

# ELDER MARK MAKABI

Considering that the Edomites *(impostor Jews)* in alliance with the European and later Caucasian hoodlums established an American legal, political, and social system of injustice with no due process for the slaves whereas the mere accusation of a slave for any crime against a Caucasian was met by death, there is little confusion that the same evil manifested in the use of terrorism of the Israelite peoples through lynchings, castration, chain gangs, etc. under the black codes of the Jim Crow.

From the beginning of the Israelite holocaust of slavery in the Americas, the sons of Esau and the American Gentile sons of Japheth maintained their languages and European system of education. Yet, these heathens made it a crime for the Israelites captives to speak their Hebrew language, Torah-rooted education, their culture, religion, and names in conjunction with prohibiting them from learning to read and write the language of their European oppressors in the land of the so-called free. The American Gentile sons of Japheth and the sons of Esau (Jewish) maintained their alien, cultural marriage ceremonies; however these enemy of true freedom made it a crime for Israelites to maintain their Israelite marriage ceremonies and outlawed Israelites from legal marriage without the permission of their oppressors whether they were slaves or free.

There is no wedding ceremony written in the Bible where a man and woman stand before a minister to pronounce them as husband and wife. The Biblical marriage ceremony began when the groom and his family went to the house of the bride, presented his dowry to the bride's father, stated the families united under God's glory, and then journeyed to their new home. Within the Biblical nation of Israel cultural wedding ceremonies did not include *jumping a broom. Jumping a broom* is a ceremony invented to symbolically unite a man and woman while under the oppression of the American sons of Japheth. However, this act was part of a deeper slave ideology that shaped the cultural identity of so-called *African-Americans* who do not know their Israelite heritage yet they sought cultural identity in maintaining their humanity and dignity which had been erased by the holocaust of slavery in the Americas.

Noting the Israelite struggle for freedom in the Americas, under the leadership of the Republicans Thaddeus Stevens and Charles Summer, conscious Caucasian men who knew the crimes against the Israelites (Negroes) in the United States, the Freedmen Bureau and the Reconstruction Acts were implemented with the intention to establish true freedom and justice. However, the anti-Semitic, racist Democratic President Andrew Johnson expressed the sentiments of most of the American Gentile sons of Japheth (Ronald Reagan, Donald Trump etc.) that the so-called "Negroes" were intellectually inferior to whites in his speech, **"The black race of Africa [is] inferior to the white man in point of intellect**." He was later impeached for his incompetence.

President Andrew Johnson much like most of his contemporaries did not have the intellectual understanding that the pigmentation does not determine race **such as the "black race."** Not all people who have darker complexions are "black" or all people with lighter complexions "white"; this is an unscrupulous invention of division by the racist Gentile sons of Japheth. The Israelite captives and later citizens in the United States alone had advanced intellectual prowess in mathematical concepts of **"equivalent value"** developed and applied superb legal capabilities **(e.g. an eye for eye)**, and served as advisors and judges for Hebraic laws since 1446 B.C. However, the American Gentile sons of Japheth applied obtuse judgment in their inept application of the slave codes and later black codes **(e.g. to cut the ears off a runaway slave for his freedom or lynch Black citizens simply for exceeding whites in commercial success, i.e. the Rosewood Massacre 1923).**

In one of President Andrew Johnson's speeches, blinded by his own ignorance, described and correctly identified the Black Americans as having **"WOOLLY-HEADED" which is relative to the description of Jesus Christ in *Revelations 1:14-15,***

*"His* **HEAD** *and his* **HAIRS** *were white like* **WOOL***, as white as snow;* and his eyes were as a flame of fire; And his **feet** like unto fine **BRASS**, as if they **burned in a furnace**;" However, the children of Israel in the United States were and remain dehumanized with word association as deplorable as the term nigger to the new euphemism "thugs"… Yet, who are the true thugs who have terrorized, robbed, raped, and killed in the name of their Christian god and the American way?

Ideally in the United States, the law was where most of the social and racial justice movements came to advocate the Israelite causes, yet the enforcement has been haphazard and social stratification based on race has kept many Israelites from their birthright as the people of God and the true builders of the American "empire". ***However, because the Israelites (so-called Negroes) have become Biblical outlaws,*** *"out-of-the-laws of the God of Israel, they have thrust themselves into the law of the lawlessness and injustice first under the slave codes, then the black codes, Jim Crow, and the evident racial injustices of the modern day.* This is why so many of the children of slavery, primarily men are in American prisons and remain in conflict with the American injustice legal institution which continues to support two societies, one privileged, one in denied complete freedom and peace in the United States and Americas.

## "Our Nation Is Moving Toward Two Societies, One Black, One White—Separate and Unequal": Excerpts from the Kerner Report 1968"

The social relevance of the slave codes and black codes among the children of slavery is the need to apply the Israelites (Biblical) law of separation to separate spiritually, culturally, and socially from the American sons of Japheth strangers and pursue true freedom through self-determination.

**Nehemiah 9:2 "And the seed of Israel separated themselves from all strangers, and stood and confessed their sins, and the iniquities of their fathers."** Our Israelite Messiah commanded the Israelite apostles (i.e. House of Israel) not to assimilate or adopt the spirituality, culture, values, and social customs of strange nations which includes the American Gentile sons of Japheth. *Matthew 10:5 "These **twelve Jesus sent forth, and commanded them, saying, GO NOT into the way of the Gentiles...:**"* We must remember that the slave codes gave power to poor White-trash Caucasians (i.e. Irish) to patrol the enslaved Israelites plantation communities and remains in residual behaviors of racist police in so-called Black neighborhoods of the United States. Nevertheless, the historical relevance of the slave codes and black codes is that the power, wealth, and prosperity of America was built on slavery under the law and a totalitarian political system that capitalized and exploited Israelite ingenuity and innovation.

The horrific effects of the slave codes and black codes enslaved the nation of Israel and violated their human righteousness **(e.g. the principles of human rights are the entitlements given by the Creator; God of Israel for all humans to excise their freedom to choice to live righteously)** that justice demands reparations from the United States government rectify and repair. In addition, the primary social and cultural relevance of the slave codes and black codes is that they altered the self-definition of race in America based on the agenda of the anti-Semitic agenda of the American Gentile sons **of Japheth** under the control of the Edomite's (Jewish peoples). The supreme rule of God's Biblical law which the Israelites refuted sealed their fate to remain in captivity for the duration of 400 years in America via the slave trade, Middle Passage, slave codes, Civil War, Reconstruction, black codes, the Back to African Movement and Pan-Africanism, Jim Crow laws, American minstrels, Harlem Renaissances, Civil Rights, the Black Power Movement, the hip-hop era, Black Lives Matter Movement, and the Second Exodus from the "American Empire" yet to come.

## AFRO-CUBANS

**Historical Highlight:** 300 Israelite captives were brought to Cuba in 1517. The Israelites could not own taverns nor could they seek asylum in the Christians' shrines, yet they were forced to convert to the heathen ways of Catholicism. They had to labor from ages of 6 to 60. We honor and remember the *Jobabo revolt (1533), Nicolas Morales (1795), Jose Aponte (1812), the "Black Seminoles"*

# BYWORD

*massacre (1816), Carlota (1843), the ten year war against Spain, Juan Gualberto Gomez, the abolishment of slavery on October 7, 1886, the 20$^{th}$ century composer, Israel López "Cachao" Valdés (the father of Afro-Cuban jazz, mambo music, and Latin pop), and all of our great and powerful Afro-Cubans Israelite ancestors that contribute to our freedom and wellbeing.*

**Origin of the name**: "The name "Cuba," an abbreviation of the indigenous word *Cubanacán,* which derives from the Taino native people words meaning *"Where fertile land is abundant".*

**Geography**: The Caribbean.

**Demographics**: An estimate 35% of the population are Israelites (*children of slavery).*

***Clarifying the blur national, racial, and color lines***: The so-called Afro-Cubans were transported in slave ships from West Africa to the Americas. Africa is a continent which has fifty-three (53) countries and was most likely named after a Phoenician prefix (Afar) and Latin suffix (ica), speaking Spanish, and classifying their national and racial identity after the name of the island which derives from Taino native people.

**Cuba:** "Where fertile land is abundant"

**Who's Your Father?** Who named Israelite's Afro-Cubans?

**In regards to your national identity, Afro-Cuban is a byword:** - Mockery

**Byword guides us back to our nation:**

    Biblical nation of Israel
    Race: Semitic
    Color of skin: Seven shades of brown
    Language: Hebrew

# ELDER MARK MAKABI

Motherland: Jerusalem, Israel

## JAMAICANS

**Historical Highlight:** Jamaica is the third largest island in the Caribbean. Great Israelite leaders such as *Marcus Garvey, Bob Marley, Harry Belafonte, Louise Bennett-Coverley, Tacky, Elder Claude and Beverly Ferguson, Usain Bolt, and Sam Sharpe* are some of Jamaica's famous heroes in the struggle for their freedom and wellbeing. The Arawak Indians were the inhabitants of the land before Columbus arrived in 1494. In 1655, the British, led by Sir William Penn (father of William Penn founder of Pennsylvania) and General Robert Venables, forced the Spanish from Jamaica. The Maroons, fought valiantly from being Hellenized by the heathen European Gentiles sons of Japheth and lived as free men and women feared by Gentiles for centuries in the countryside and mountains. The international economy was rooted in the triangular trade between Arabs, Africans (Hamites), the Caribbean colonists, and Europe. The Europeans manufactured goods based on Israelite slave labor and ingenuity. Sugar brought about commercial and economic prosperity. Slavery was abolished in 1834. Jamaica became independent in 1962.

**Origin of the name**: Xaymacor, Hamaica named derives from the Arawak-Taino word which means "land of wood and water."

**Geography**: Caribbean.

**Demographics**: An estimate 97.4% of the population is Israelites *(descendant of slaves)*

*Clarifying the blur national, racial, and color lines*: The so-called Jamaicans were transported in slave ships from West Africa to the Americas. Africa is a continent which has fifty-three (53) *countries and was most likely named after a Phoenician prefix and Latin suffix, speaking English, and classifying their national and racial identity after the name of the island which derives from the Arawak's and Tainos Language.*

**Reggae music:** Originated in Jamaica in the 1960s.

**Jamaica**: The land of wood and water

**Who's Your Father?** Who named Israelite's Jamaicans?

**In regards to your national identity, Jamaican is a byword:**
- Ridicule

**Byword guides us back to our nation:**

    Biblical nation of Israel

    Race: Semitic

    Pigmentation: Seven shades of blackness

    Language: Hebrew

    Homeland: Jerusalem, Israel

## CREOLE

**Historical Highlight:** During the colonial era, the term "creole" represented descends from French, Spanish, or Portuguese settlers not from the mainland country. However, in modern times "creole" has various meaning to different people in different places. Moreover, creole was a label to distinguish the children of intermarriages between *Native Americans and Europeans, Israelite slaves and Native Americans*, and/or *a combination of Israelite, Native American, and European peoples.*

**Origin of the name**: Creole (***criollo***) from the *Latin "creare"* to ***create, beget,*** or ***mixture. Crioulo,*** a Portuguese word which means ***"slave born in a master's house,"*** or ***"New World slave of***

*so-called African descent";* however, *"Criollo"* is Spanish for identification with mixed ancestry.

**Geography**: primarily the Caribbean, Louisiana United States of America, and Belize.

**Demographics**: An estimate of individuals who identify as Creoles of so-called African descent in the Americas is not known.

***Clarifying the blur national, racial, and color lines****: The so-called Creoles were transported in slave ships from West Africa to the Americas. Africa is a continent which has fifty-three (53) countries and was most likely named after a Phoenician prefix (Afar) and Latin suffix (ica), speaking dialects from English, French, Portuguese, Taino, Arawak, West African, Dutch, and Spanish languages, and classifying their national and racial identity from a various Europeans meaning "slave born in a master's house", mixture. "beget" a "creation".*

**Creole**: The mixture came primarily through the Portuguese, French, and Spanish raping the enslaved Israelite woman. In the United States, "creole" is usually synonymous with mixed people of Louisiana with African descent *(the Israelite slaves, French, Native Americans, Spanish, and later the Haitian immigrants that migrated following Haitian independence).*

**Who's Your Father?** Who named Israelite's Creoles?

**In regards to your national identity, Creole is a byword:**
- Mockery

**Byword guides us back to our nation:**
    Biblical nation of Israel
    Race: Semitic
    Color of skin: Seven shades of brown

# BYWORD

Language: Hebrew
Motherland: Jerusalem, Israel

## AFRO-MEXICANS

**Historical Highlight**: The children of Israel have made enormous contributions to Mexico and the Americas. Furthermore, **Juan Cortes**  is believed to be the first Israelite slave brought to Mexico with the conquistador "Herman Cortes" in 1519. Israelites slaves worked on the sugar plantations in horrendous conditions of coastal Veracruz. In 1570, the great Israelite spiritual leader and general, **Gaspar Yanga** led a rebellion against the Spanish and established a Palenque or settlement of self-emancipated slaves near the town of Cordoba. The town of Yanga, recognized as a "free settlement" remained undisturbed by the Spanish for 40 years. Yanga's legacy is a remarkable achievement; he is also referred to as "The First Liberator of the Americas".

*Mexico's second president, "Vicente Guerrero"* was an Israelite, (Black man) labeled as a mulatto. He was a hero of Mexico's War of Independence from Spain. Guerrero abolished slavery in 1829.

**Origin of the name:** Origin of the name Mexico is derived from the Aztec god of war, Huitzilopochtli also known as Mextli. Mextli was associated with the moon.

**Geography**: Central America.

**Demographics**: An estimate 0.1% of the population is Israelites *(descendant of slaves).*

***Clarifying the blur national, racial, and color lines:*** *The so-called Afro-Mexicans were transported in slave ships from West Africa to the Americas. Africa is a continent which has fifty-three (53) countries and was most likely named after a Phoenician prefix and Latin suffix, speaking the Spanish language, and classifying their national and racial identity from a word that derives from the name for the Aztec god of war.*

**Mexico**: derived from the Aztec god of war, Huitzilopochtli also known as Mextli. Mextli was associated with the moon.

**Mexican Minstrels:** Mexico celebrates a racist icon named **"Memin Pinguin"**

**Who's Your Father?** Who named Israelite's Afro-Mexicans?

**In regards to your national identity, Afro-Mexican is a by-word:** - Ridicule

**Byword guides us back to our nation:**
  Biblical nation of Israel
  Race: Semitic
  Pigmentation: Seven shades of blackness
  Language: Hebrew
  Homeland: Jerusalem, Israel

## COLORED PEOPLE

**Origin of the name**: The origin of this byword is obscured; however it is believed the term "colored" was documented during the administration of President John Tyler in 1844. The term "colored people" became virtually universal in the national identification of the Israelites captives and later citizens of America until the 1960s when Black and later Afro/African American were used in the 1970s, '80s, and so on. Colored has been used in association with the **Massachusetts 54*th* Colored Infantry and the N.A.A.C.P., the** *National Association for the Advancement of Colored People.*

**Geography**: primarily the United States.

**Demographics**: An estimate of 25 million Israelites in the United States.

*Clarifying the blur national, racial, and color lines: The so-called coloreds were transported in slave ships from West Africa to the Americas. Africa is a continent which has fifty-three (53) countries and was most likely named after a Phoenician prefix (Afar) and Latin suffix (ica), speaking various European languages, and classifying their national and racial identity as a color of colors.*

**Colored**: A person belonging to a racial group not categorized as the color white.

**White**: is a color not a race.

**Leprosy:** Did you know having so-called "white" (i.e. reddish) skin, blond hair, red hair, and blue or green eyes is considered a genetic disorder and curse according to the Bible? In addition, the European Gentile sons of Japheth in relation to their texture of hair, reddish, pale or colorless skin, and various eye colors are considered to be mutants or individuals who adapted to colder environments in the northern hemisphere, originating from the first true human beings, the people of Black Asiatic. Based on less Vitamin D production in higher latitudes (leading to lower bone density, challenged pulmonary and skin health, and the need for calcium sources such as cow milk) and changes in diet (less nutritious food sources) in

Eurasia, pale skin, Albino, related hair texture, and eye color came about some 7,000 to 10,000 years ago.

**Numbers 12:9-10** "and the anger of the LORD was kindled against them; and he departed. And the cloud departed from off the tabernacle; and, behold, Miriam became **LEPROUS, WHITE AS SNOW**: and Aaron looked upon Miriam, and, behold, she was leprous."

**Who's Your Father?** Who named Israelite's colored people?

**In regards to your national identity, colored people is a byword:** - Mockery

**Byword guides us back to our nation:**
   Biblical nation of Israel
   Race: Semitic
   Color of skin: Seven shades of brown
   Language: Hebrew
   Motherland: Jerusalem, Israel

## MONTSERRATIANS

**Historical Highlight**: This island became one of the symbols of Christian Americas hypocrisy because it was a refuge for European Catholics escaping religious persecutions. These European Christians would play a major role in the captivity of the Israelites. The Irish first came as indentured servants; later, the Israelites captives were brought with yokes around their necks in the 1660s. The Irish community discovered a plan for slave insurrection that would have taken place on St. Patrick Day; nine slaves were hanged. Woe unto the Irish! The price of sugar declined on the world market, and the Montserrat plantation system fell after slavery was abolished in 1834.

**Origin of the name**: Christopher Columbus, named the island

# BYWORD

"Santa Maria de Monsterrate" (1493) because it remind him of the Black virgin of Montserrate shrine in Spain which literally means "Jagged Mountain."

**Geography**: Caribbean.

**Demographics**: An estimate of 90% of the populations is Israelites which includes so-called mulattos (*the descendant of slaves*).

***Clarifying the blur national, racial, and color lines***: *The so-called Montserratians were transported in slave ships from West Africa to the Americas. Africa is a continent which has fifty-three (53) countries and was most likely named after a Phoenician prefix and Latin suffix, speaking the English language, and classifying their national and racial identity after a name coined by Christopher Columbus based on a shrine of the "Black" Virgin Mary in Spain.*

**Montserrat:** *A shrine, "Santa Maria de Monsterrate", a statue of the Virgin Mary, depicted as a true (Black Biblical) Israelite woman.*

**Black Madonna:** Did the Europeans elite know that the Biblical "Virgin Mary" was a Black woman? Why did the shrine of Montserrat have a statue of a Black virgin woman? Santa Maria means Saint Mary. **Who's Your Father?** Who named Israelite's Montserratians?

**In regards to your national identity, Montserratian is a byword:** - Ridicule

**Byword guides us back to our nation:**
- Biblical nation of Israel
- Race: Semitic
- Pigmentation: Seven shades of blackness
- Language: Hebrew
- Homeland: Jerusalem, Israel

## ELDER MARK MAKABI

### AFRO-CURACAONS

**Historical Highlight:** Curacao's (Korsow) was considered the largest transport center for slaves in the so-called New World. Curacao had no plantations and was a distribution center for Israelites captives. By 1660, Israelite captives began arriving weekly to be brainwashed, beaten, and bought by major slave trading companies that supplied them to numerous European colonies. In 1795, there was a slave revolt led by *"Tula"* and his brothers. They are Israelite freedom fighters essential to the history of Curacao. The *Museum Kura Hulanda* (a museum noting Israelite slavery in Curacao) was built by *Dr. Jacob Gelt Dekker* in 1998; however, Israelites should exclusively have control in sharing and expressing their history concerning the Israelite Biblical holocaust of slavery.

**Origin of the name**: There are several theories of the origin of the name; however, none can be proven conclusively. One theory is that the name derived from the "Caiquetio" Indian language, or another theory is that the word derives from the Spanish word for heart "corazon" or Portuguese "curazon" similar to the English word "core"; however, in 1525, the Spanish refer to the island as "Curaacote," or "Curasaore".

**Geography**: The Caribbean; largest of the six islands comprising the Netherlands Antiles: Curacao, Bonaire, St. Martin, Saba, St. Eustatius, and Aruba.

**Demographics**: An estimate of 85% of the populations is Israelites which includes descendants of intermarriages *(the descendant of slaves)*.

*Clarifying the blur national, racial, and color lines*: The so-called Afro-Curacaons were transported in slave ships from West

# BYWORD

*Africa to the Americas. Africa is a continent which has fifty-three (53) countries and was most likely named after a Phoenician prefix (Afar) and Latin suffix (ica), speaking the Dutch, English, and Spanish languages, and classifying their national and racial identity after the name of the island which has numerous origin theories and most likely is believed to be a derivative of the Spanish word "corazon".*

**Curacao *(Korsow)*:** Could derive from "Caiquetio", Portuguese, "curazon", or Spanish "corazon" (heart, core)**.**

**Yui-di Korsow:** "Child from Curacao", refers to the Afro-Curacaons.

**Who's Your Father?** Who named Israelite's Afro-Curacaons?

**In regards to your national identity, Afro-Curacaon is a byword:** - Mockery

**Byword guides us back to our nation:**

    Biblical nation of Israel

    Race: Semitic

    Color of skin: Seven shades of brown

    Language: Hebrew

    Motherland: Jerusalem, Israel

## AFRO-VENEZUELANS

**Historical Highlight**: In 1528, Israelite captives arrived with their scientific, legal, engineering, medical, culinary, agriculture, musical, artisan, rich-culture, and other essential skills to build the Americas. In 1532, there were slave revolts in Coro. Later, in 1553, *El Negro Miguel, Michael the Black, later known as El Rey Miguel (King Michael) led a successful revolt* in the Buria mines and undermined the Europeans institution of slavery. In 1721, Captain

## Elder Mark Makabi

Juan Del Rosario Blanco established the only legally recognized "free town" in Curiepe, Barlovento. In 1770, legendary Cimarron, Guillermon Rivas established Ocoyta, a cumbe (Mandingo for "free town") for freed and/or self-emancipated slaves (runaways). Slavery was abolished in 1854. **Pedro Camejo**, a Venezuelan War for Independence hero, was the first Black man to fight with recognition for his efforts. He was immortalized as the First Black Man [of Venezuela] as "El Negro Primero".

**Origin of the name**: Derives from the Italian Venezuela meaning "Little Venice." The Indians had houses on stilts above the river current, which reminded the Italian explorer Amerigo Vespucci and Spanish explorer Alonso de Ojeda of the houses in Venice.

**Geography**: South America.

**Demographics**: An estimate of 10-26.5 % of the populations are Israelites, including intermarriages *(the descendant of slaves)*.

*Clarifying the blur national, racial, and color lines*: *The so-called Afro-Venezuelans were transported in slave ships from West Africa to the Americas. Africa is a continent which has fifty-three (53) countries and was most likely named after a Phoenician prefix and Latin suffix, speaking the Spanish language, and classifying their national and racial identity after the name of an Italian city, Venice.*

**Venezuela:** Named after Venice, Italy.

**Minstrel Celebration:** Barranquilla Carnival **"El Negrita Puloy"**

**Who's Your Father?** Who named Israelite's Afro-Black Venezuelans?

**In regards to your national identity, Afro-Venezuelan is a byword:** - Ridicule

# BYWORD

**Byword guides us back to our nation:**
    Biblical nation of Israel
    Race: Semitic
    Pigmentation: Seven shades of blackness
    Language: Hebrew
    Homeland: Jerusalem, Israel

## MAROONS

**Historical Highlight**: The Maroons reminds us of our great Maccabeus forefathers who led forces against the Seleucid Greeks and re-established the sanctity of our temple in 164 B.C. In 1690, Cudjoe, a great Israelite leader, led the Maroons to freedom. The  resolve of the Maroons is a testimony to the Israelites superior character to win against all odds. In addition, the Maroons were able to build and established their own independent communities. The communities became a refuge for escaped Israelite slaves. The Maroons made alliances with Sir France Drake to fight the Spanish. Also, the Maroons forced the British into agreeing to treaties in the Israelites' favor. The Maroons played a vital role in the history of the *Americas (i.e. Brazil, Suriname, Puerto Rico, Jamaica, Haiti, St. Vincent, the Dominican Republic, and Cuba)*. The Maroons are national and international Israelite heroes.

**Origin of the name**: Spanish named the Israelites who escaped from bondage "fugitives" or "runaway slaves."

**Geography**: The Caribbean and South America.

**Demographics**: A remnant of the 12 tribes of Israel scattered in the Americas.

***Clarifying the blur national, racial, and color lines***: *The so-called Maroons were transported in slave ships from West Africa to the Americas. Africa is a continent which has fifty-three (53) countries and was most likely named after a Phoenician prefix (Afar) and Latin suffix (ica), speaking various European languages, and classifying their national and racial identity from a Spanish word.*

**Proverbs 3:31** "Envy thou not the oppressor, and choose none of his ways"

**Maroon: English (Spanish corruption):** Spanish for "runaway slaves" or "fugitives".

**Who's Your Father?** Who named Israelite's Maroons?

**In regards to your national identity, Maroon is a byword:**
- Mockery

**Byword guides us back to our nation:**
Biblical nation of Israel
Race: Semitic
Color of skin: Seven shades of brown
Language: Hebrew
Motherland: Jerusalem, Israel

## AFRO-HONDURANS

**Historical Highlight**: The Israelite holocaust of slavery is a history of violence, injustices, racism, discrimination, rape, marginalization, revolts, dehumanization, and a testimony of our superior character. The Israelite slaves arrived in 1540; however, many escaped and intermarried with native people and were known as *"castas."* In addition, the bay land area of Honduras is the location to where the Garifuna (Black Caribs) were exiled by British after numerous battles. The revolt at the Bay of Honduras in 1773 was one of the most formidable thus **Chief *"Satuye"*** is a national and international Israelite hero who died in battle fighting the British in St. Vincent In 1795. When the British regained St. Vincent, they expelled the Garifuna rebels to the island of Roatan in the Bay of Honduras; many died of yellow fever and starvation. The island is a symbol of Garifuna culture and Honduran freedom. He inspired Garifuna revolts in Honduras and later Belize (British Honduras). Slavery was abolished in 1838.

**Origin of the name**: Columbus named the country "Honduras", Spanish for "depths" which refers to the nation's deep waters.

**Geography**: Central America.

**Demographics**: An estimate of 2% of the population is Israelites (*descendant of slaves*).

*Clarifying the blur national, racial, and color lines*: *The so-called Afro-Hondurans were transported in slave ships from West Africa to the Americas. Africa is a continent which has fifty-three (53) countries and was most likely named after a Phoenician prefix and Latin suffix, speaking the Spanish language, and classifying their national and racial identity from a Spanish word for "depths" that was named by an Italian.*

**Honduras:** "Depths"

**Who's Your Father?** Who named Israelite's Afro-Black Hondurans?

**In regards to your national identity, Afro-Honduran is a**

# Elder Mark Makabi

**byword:** - Ridicule

**Byword guides us back to our nation:**

Biblical nation of Israel
Race: Semitic
Pigmentation: Seven shades of blackness
Language: Hebrew
Homeland: Jerusalem, Israel

## ONE DROP RULES!

*My bloodline flows from the Hebrews,*
*the seed of Abraham, his color hue,*
*The exclusive bloodline of the blessed,*
*One Drop Rules, Negro Blood Rules,*

*My blood flows from Sarah the mother of our Israelite nation*
*& keeper of Isaac's covenant,*
*One Drop Rules, Israelite Blood Rules!*

*My blood flows from the heritage of Jacob to Israel,*
*One Drop Rules, Negro Blood Rules!*

*My blood flows from the legacy of Joseph's reign in Egypt,*
*One Drop Rules, Israelite Blood Rules!*

*My blood flows from the heritage of Queen Esther's virtuousness,*
*One Drop Rules, Negro Blood Rules,*

## BYWORD

*My blood flows from the legacy of King David's Psalms,*
*One Drop Rules, Israelite Blood Rules,*

*My blood flows from the smoke of the Israelite Apostles,*
*One Drop Rules, Negro Blood Rules,*

*One Drop is potent,*
*One Drop defines,*
*One Drop designs the DNA lines,*

*One Drop dominates,*
*One Drop dictates,*
*One Drop terminates,*
*One Drop germinates,*

*One Drop detracts inferior genetics to Negro, Spanish for black,*
*One drop produces the spices of our rhythmic soul,*
*Gospel, Reggae, Jazz, Hip-hop, Rumba, Salsa,*
*Disco, & Calypso*

*One drop is blessed,*
*One drop is pure,*
*One drop is feared.*
*One drop is revered,*

*One drop produced the Messiah,*
*An Israelite kin, the holy blood to cleanses our sin,*

## CHAPTER 5
# BYWORD

## "A Nation Called Out of Their Name"

Names and the naming of our children was central to our Hebrew cultural traditions and spirituality whereas the cultural significances of the parents naming their children was to establish their authority and legacy. In addition, the spirituality of the names that were selected for our child and our method of making that selection set forth their purpose in life. The God of Israel established His authority over His creation when He named the things He created. The power in naming established the purpose of everything God created. The God of Israel named our Hebrew forbearers, Abraham, Sarah, Isaac, and changed *Jacob's* name ("He who supplants, tracks, or follows") to *Israel* in the process of establishing His chosen nation, the Children of Israel. Thus, Israel is a name of a black man which means a "Prince, Favored by God, God perseveres". And as God's chosen, Israel and his children have the power to live godly in an ungodly world; **"ites"** refers to the children of. *(E.g. Israel-ites the children of Israel, Cannan-ites the children of Cannan).* In addition to the descendants of Israel, the promise land was named after our father Israel.

Israel is the name that the Heavenly Father gave His chosen people *(the descendant of slaves in Egypt and later the Americas)* as their national identity, establish God's parental authority through covenants, judgments, and blessings. Thus, the offering up of our children unto the Lord **(as Kunta Kinte's father, Omoro Kinte, does in the classic TV mini-series, Roots, 1977)** is our Israelite culture and specific instructions the Heavenly Father gave us in the process of giving our children Biblical Hebrew names. However, because the Israelites turned from their Heavenly Father to go whoring with the gods of the heathens, our Heavenly Father disowned us. This led to our downfall in civil wars, ruin, captivity, and the American Gentile sons of Japheth establishing their authority by naming, de-naming, and renaming the Israelites during slavery in the Americas.

One of the most horrifying atrocities of our **Israelite Biblical holocaust of slavery in the Americas** was the removing of our Hebrew names and replacing them with alien, Gentile names that would initiate the formation of the bastardization of the Biblical nation of Israel in the Americas. *Moreover, the dismantling of our Israelite families and erasing of our culture, symbols, holy days, religion, history, rituals, wedding ceremonies, spirituality, and Hebrew language would eventually lead* to a **nation that would be called out of their name**. However, the American legal, political, psychological, and social process of how such an astonishing atrocity occurred is rooted in the sacred covenant between the Most High and the Israelites *(descendant of slaves)* in keeping their word of honor, their covenants with the God of Israel. However, the Biblical nation of Israel agreed to the consequences of being *"called out"* when they dishonored their word to God. Moreover, when men and women honor their word they express the ideals of love, respect, value for self, community, their name, family, culture, and nation. However, when men and women develop a reputation for dishonoring their word, they begin to be **called out of their name** (e.g. he or she is a "jive turkey") by their peers.

In sundry times, too many rebellious Israelites begin to develop unprincipled characteristics which were contrary to their sacred principles, leading to the reduction of the Biblical nation of Israel to a byword; this undermined the underlying code of when sacred principles are honored by a nation the nation is steadfast, strong, and regimented. With precision, the prophet Moses **called out how** the Biblical nation of Israel would be *"called out"* if they breached their sacred covenant and if they disregarded the responsibility of taking ownership of their Biblical inheritance as a sovereign nation. The Most High and his servants, the prophet, Moses and the high priest, Aaron, expected the Israelites to understand their concept of freedom and become servants unto God **(e.g. to be free is to serve)**. Freedom is its own reward; in order to be free there is a need for *moral order* **(i.e. the laws governing of freedom)** that puts in place means to agree and thrive; thus the Law was given unto Moses. The nature of freedom expresses the power and majesty of freedom based on function and/or application; even in nature, the sun, moon, day, night, seasons, rain, stars, etc. continue freedom yet must adhere to the laws of physics to exist and remain functional in the physical world such is the freedom given unto us by God. The responsibility and the reward of freedom are reciprocal. Therefore, the price for the freedom of the Israelites from Egyptian bondage was to serve the God of Israel. **Exodus 7:16 "And thou shalt say unto him, The Lord God of the Hebrews hath sent me unto thee, saying, LET MY PEOPLE GO, that they may SERVE me in the wilderness: and, behold, hitherto thou wouldest not hear."**

    The Israelites had a choice to be free to serve the *God of their Hebrew fathers Abraham, Isaac, and Jacob* or to be slaves to their enemies. Moreover, if they chose to be slaves, they would learn how to serve with excellence as ***"house negroes"*** (i.e. the character Stephen in the movie Django 2012). Nevertheless, the process of how the Biblical nation of Israel would be called out of their name and be reduced to a byword began with the Israelites choosing between the rewards of blessings for obedience or consequences of forsaking their sacred covenant and adopting the pagan customs of the heathens. **Moreover, the historical account of the holocaust of slavery in the Americas and the temporary transfer of ownership of the Biblical nation of Israel to alien nations led to a barbaric system of naming, de-naming, and the re-naming of the Hebrew slaves in the Americas.** However, one of the fundamental process to dehumanize the Israelites as slaves in the Americas was forcing them to abandon their Hebrew names and rename themselves with Arabic, European, and/or names based on their regional location under occupation power alien powers such as Nigeria, from Latin "niger" meaning "black", but associated with derogatory terms such as "nigger" ***(related to other epithets*** *such as **Sambo, coon, Uncle Tom,** etc.)* during the transatlantic slave trade in the Americas.

In the mid-15th century, when the European Gentile sons of Japheth began their invasions and later occupations of Africa and began the *Transatlantic Slave Trade*, they begin branding the Israelite captives on their body parts with hot irons like cattle and baptized them into the religion of slavery. The point of the branding originated with the Royal African Company as a standard model to indicate the transfer of ownership of the sovereign, Biblical nation of Israel to the property of a heathen Japhetic state. Branding of the Israelite captives disfigured their shoulders or breasts, which was deemed a receipt of sale of slaves. Brands usually represented points of origin in connection with the "company" that bought them and the ship in which they arrived in the Americas.

In 1607, King Phillip III of Spain established the practice for Israelite captives to be given Christian names and baptism as a means to subjugate versus liberate the children of Israel in the Americas. In West Africa, the Israelite captives would be taken to one of the six Christian shrines or in the main square with a Christian priest to perform the pagan baptism into the religion slavery. This transformation of the Israelites through the process of Christian pagan baptism, assigning Israelites with Christian names, sprinkling salt on their tongues, providing them with so-called holy water, using hot iron branding, and documenting the Israelites under new alien slave names was not only demoralizing it was the destruction of our glory and denial of our true legacy. Upon arrival in the Americas, the Israelite slaves were forbidden to exercise their human rights in retaining their Hebrew names and the naming customs thereof *(i.e.*

## BYWORD

***Kunta Knite is bastardized by his renaming of Toby, Roots, TV mini-series, 1977).***

It was not until after the American Civil War that the Israelites had the legal right to name their children as citizens (de jure) of the United States. *Thus, the naming, de-naming, and the re-naming of the Israelite slaves was a process for the slave masters to erase the Israelite identity of the slaves and maintain social, cultural, political, spiritual, economical, and psychological hegemony over the slaves and later second-class citizens.* This was and continues to be accomplished by reducing the Israelites to *nonpersons*, using derogatory bywords and pejoratives such as *Negro, Colored, wench, boy, coon, and nigger,* and applying the labeling theory of *"self-fulfilling's prophecy", the psychological mechanisms that keep many Israelite men and women in psychological bondage, today.* Moreover, the descendant of slaves who recklessly promote, support, glorify, bywords such as **"*Nigger*"** and/or refer to themselves and their people as niggers or niggas are vomiting dung on their Israelite heritage, ancestors, the holocaust of slavery in the Americas, further affirming that that they are nonpersons. This pathological behavior only validates the ongoing stigmatization and the horrific treatment of the descendant of slaves in the Americas *(e.g. Emmett Till, Eric Gardner, Sandra Bland, Sean Bell, Trayvon Martin, Mike Brown-the Ferguson, MO murder, the human rights violations of the Afro-Colombians, Afro-Brazilians, Afro-Cubans, Jamaicans, Afro-Latinos, and many more).*

The duality of being "called out" for blessings or curses in modern American society is a primary cultural and social expression to challenge, confront, provoke, and invoke disgrace on one person, family, place, thing, or honor. The spiritual implications for Israelites being **"called out"** was to invoke a profound humiliation for profaning the holy name of the Most High and spewing dung on their Israelite (Biblical) inheritance from God. This was a result of the Israelites disinheriting their sacred covenant. Even to this very day, many confused and lost children of Israel continue to choose being called **niggers over Israelites**, choosing to be the **tail and not the head**. This is the **house Negro** choosing so-called equality over being blessed above all nations. This is the **coon** choosing Caucasian-defined "civil rights" over the Exodus to their Promise Land. This is the **"boy"** choosing to be the **child and not the father**. This is the m**ammy** choosing to be the masters slave wench over being the virtuous woman for her husband, children, and her household. This is sad and **astonishing.**

Nevertheless, the good news is that the Most High revealed His magnificent plan for redeeming the Israelites which I characterize as *"The Blessings of the Curse."* How can a curse be a blessing? It is like learning a deeper lesson from a grave mistake. The Most High would use the curse as a blessing in the latter days as a process for the healing, empowerment, unity, self-determination, prosperity, peace, celebration, self-edification, and liberation of the Biblical nation of Israel. As bywords were used to dehumanize Israelites, the pain and degradation attached to them would and continues to empower them through self-knowledge and spiritual enlightenment.

Growing out of pain, a people united grow stronger. Bywords were used as racist epithets to socially, psychologically, racially, culturally, economically, and spiritually devalue the humanity of the Israelite captives; yet, from this many of us who know ourselves as the children of Israel have begun a journey of healing. Bywords separated our families, undermined our freedom, led us deeper into European-Caucasians-created chaos in the attempt to continue a totalitarian socio-political system; however, the children of Israel know their true names, know their true legacy, and know they are free. They do not continue to ask for what is their God-given blessing and birthright.

> DEUTERONOMY 28:37 (NIV)
> "You will become a thing of horror, a **BYWORD** and an object of ridicule among all the peoples where the Lord will drive you".

## U.S. VIRGIN ISLANDERS

**Historical Highlight**: Columbus sighted the island in 1493; however, the island was divided between the English and Danish. The United States Virgin Islands or U.S.V.I.'s history consists of a plantation economy, criminal pirates, and rum. Two major events shaped the island history when the French sold St. Croix to the Danish and a massive slave revolt on St. John Island resulted in the Israelites taking control of the island for six months. Slavery was abolished in 1848.

**Origin of the name**: The mass murderer, Christopher Columbus, named this island he presumptuously *called "Saint Ursula"after the supposed Romano-British, Christian martyr* and her 11,000 martyred virgins and in reference to a Roman pagan feast day of the dead on October 21st. Supposedly on a pilgrimage through Europe, in the city of Cologne, Ursula and her virgins were beheaded by the savage Attila the Hun.

## Elder Mark Makabi

**Geography**: Caribbean (consisting of St. Croix, St. John, and St. Thomas islands)

**Demographics**: An estimate of 79.7% of the population are Israelites *(the descendant of slaves).*

***Clarifying the blur national, racial, and color lines:*** *The so-called Virgin Islanders were transported in slave ships from West Africa to the Americas. Africa is a continent which has fifty-three (53) countries and was most likely named after a Phoenician prefix (Afar) and Latin suffix (ica), speaking the English language, and classifying their national and racial identity after the name of the island that an Italian named after a legendary, more than likely mythical, Romano-British princess.*

**U.S. Virgin Islander:** Named after Ursula and her 11,000 martyred virgins.

**Who's Your Father?** Who named Israelite's U.S. Virgin Islanders?

**In regards to your national identity, Virgin Islander is a byword:** Mockery

**Byword guides us back to our nation:**
>Biblical nation of Israel
>Race: Semitic
>Pigmentation: Seven shades of blackness
>Language: Hebrew
>Homeland: Jerusalem, Israel

## BARBADIANS

**Historical Highlight:** The island was inhabited by the Arawaks natives. The Israelite captives made Barbados a prosperous land. An

## BYWORD

**Who's Your Father?** Who named Israelite's Afro-Uruguayans?

**In regards to your national identity, Afro-Uruguayan is a byword:** Ridicule

**Byword guides us back to our nation:**
>  Biblical nation of Israel
>  Race: Semitic
>  Color of skin: Seven shades of brown
>  Language: Hebrew
>  Motherland: Jerusalem, Israel

### VINCENTIANS

**Historical Highlight:** The birth place of the "**Black Caribs**" or **"Garifuna"** *(Israelites intermarriages with the natives)*. In 1675 a Dutch ship with the European colonists and Israelite captives wrecked in the waters. The Israelite captives were the only survivors. The Kalipunas welcomed the Israelites and intermarried; they became known as the "Black Caribs." *The so-called yellow Caribs are considered to be pure Carib or Kalipunas descent.* St. Vincent became a refuge for escaped Israelite slaves. The self-emancipated Israelites defended their land from the Europeans intruders. However, from 1627 to 1796, the French established a settlement and used Israelite slave labor to produce sugar, tobacco, and cotton. Eventually, in 1796, the British would control the island; later, they deported the *"Black Caribs"* to Roatan Island of the coast of Honduras (which they later claimed as Belize).

**Origin of the name**: Christopher Columbus named this island after a man named Vincent that the Gentiles Europeans presumptu-

## ELDER MARK MAKABI

ously called "Saint" in honor of a pagan "Feast for Vincent" (1498).

**Geography**: Caribbean.

**Demographics**: An estimate of 85% of the population are *Israelites (descendant of slaves including the Grenadines).*

*Clarifying the blur national, racial, and color lines: The so-called Vincentians were transported in slave ships from West Africa to the Americas. Africa is a continent which has fifty-three (53) countries and was most likely named after a Phoenician prefix (Afar) and Latin suffix (ica), speaking English and the French patois dialect, and classifying their national and racial identity after the name of the island that was named by an Italian who he named after a French man.*

**St. Vincent:** A man name Vincent who the Gentiles presumptuously called a saint. The Children of Israel are the Saints (Psalm 148:14)

**Who's Your Father?** Who named Israelite's Vincentians?

**In regards to your national identity, Vincentian is a byword:** Mockery

**Byword guides us back to our nation:**
    Biblical nation of Israel
    Race: Semitic
    Pigmentation: Seven shades of blackness
    Language: Hebrew
    Homeland: Jerusalem, Israel

### AFRICAN AMERICANS

**Historical Highlight**: From 1619 to the present, the Israelites (so-called African-Americans) had demonstrated extraordinary estimated 40,000 slaves arrived during the Middle Passage (1640). The first slaves in Barbados were Irish sons of Japheth, known today as the "Red Legs"; however, the Irish were indentured servants and knew their names and retained their identity. They suffered nothing like the children of Israel in the Americas. Governor Humphrey Walrond issued that Israelites and Indians were perpetual slaves, never to be considered for indentured servitude only indefinite slavery.

The most noticeable Israelites from Barbados was *Tituba, a female slave, sold and transferred to Massachusetts. In 1692, Tituba* was accused, tried, convicted, and executed during the infamous *"Salem Witch Trials"*. The great Israelite Bussa led one of longest slave revolts in history on April 14, 1816. This insurrection called to order odd alliance between the Israelites and the Irish, leading to a revolution. One description of the penalties slaves faced for insubordination to insurrections were "nailing them down on the ground with crooked sticks on every limb, and then applying the fire by degrees from feet and hands, burning them gradually up to the head, whereby their pains are extravagant." The European criminals could claim a reimbursement from the government of 25 pounds per slave executed as if it were insurance.

**Origin of the name**: It is believed that in 1536, the Portuguese explorer, Pedro A. Campos, named this island "Barbados", which means "The Bearded Ones", based on the fichus trees' long roots which resembled beards.

**Geography**: Caribbean.

**Demographics**: An estimate 90% of the population is Israelites.

***Clarifying the blur national, racial, and color lines***: *The so-called Barbadians were transported in slave ships from West Africa* to the Americas. *Africa is a continent which has fifty-three (53) countries and was most likely named after a Phoenician prefix and Latin suffix, speaking the English language and classifying their national and racial identity after the name of the island which was named by a Portuguese explorer.*

**Barbados:** "Bearded Ones"

**Who's Your Father?** Who named Israelite's Barbadians?

**In regards to your national identity, Barbadian is a byword:** Ridicule

**Byword guides us back to our nation:**
 Biblical nation of Israel
 Race: Semitic
 Color of skin: Seven shades of brown
 Language: Hebrew
 Motherland: Jerusalem, Israel

## AFRO-COSTA RICANS

**Historical Highlight:** The Spanish shipped Israelites from the coast of West Africa in the 16th century to replace the Native Americans as slaves. Israelites captives were isolated on farm plantations from the rest of the country and intermarried with the Indians creating the so-called "Zambos" akin to the pejorative "Sambo". In 1821, Costa Rica won independence from Spain, which led to slavery being abolished on April 17, 1824. In 1871, the Israelites built the railroads and worked for the *Untied Standard Fruit Company on banana plantations. The United Standard Fruit Company is now called Chiquita.* Even though Israelites improved their economic status by working their farms efficiently, they were not considered citizens of Costa Rica and did not possess legal rights to own land. However, many Ticos *(Caucasians)* moved into Israelites regions and took over the land.

**Origins of name:** The name "Rich Coast" is attributed to Columbus' (1502) and/or Gil Gonzalez' (1522) voyages and view of the land because both so-called explorers observed the abundance gold ornaments the Indians were wearing before they subjugated them and either enslaved or massacred them.

**Geography**: Central America.

**Demographics**: Estimated 3% of the populations are Israelites *(descendant of slaves).*

***Clarifying the blur national, racial, and color lines****: The so-called Afro-Costa Ricans were transported in slave ships from West Africa to the Americas. Africa is a continent which has fifty-three (53) countries and was most likely named after a Phoenician prefix (Afar) and Latin suffix (ica), speaking the Spanish language and classifying their national and racial identity after the land an Italian and/or Spanish named based on observing the richly adorned Native Central Americans.*

**Costa Rica:** Rich Coast.

**Who's Your Father?** Who named Israelite's Afro-Costa Ricans?

**In regards to your national identity, Afro-Costa Rican is a byword:** Mockery

**Byword guides us back to our nation:**
    Biblical nation of Israel
    Race: Semitic
    Pigmentation: Seven shades of blackness

# ELDER MARK MAKABI

Language: Hebrew
Homeland: Jerusalem, Israel

## AFRO-URUGUAYANS

**Historical Highlight:** In 1680, the "Invisible Israelites" of Uruguay were brought to the Americas by the Portuguese. In addition, Israelite captives 'contributions were essential to the infrastructure, economy, social nuisances, spirituality, and culture of Uruguay. *Juan Cortes, and Juan Garrido* were conquerors with the murderous Hernan Cortes. *Juan Vallenle* sailed with Pedro de Valdivia, lieutenant under Pizarro of Peru and the first royal governor of Chile. **José Gervasio Artigas** and **Manuel Oribe** were valiant Israelite soldiers. The tango dance originated with the Israelites captives of Uruguay. Slavery was abolished in 1842.

**Origin of the name**: Uruguay derives from the fact that the country lies east of the Uruguay River. *Uruguay* is a Guaraní word meaning "river of shellfish," or "river from which the uru birds come."

**Geography**: South America – The Eastern Republic of Uruguay

**Demographics**: An estimate of 5.9% of the population is Israelites *(descendant of slaves)*.

*Clarifying the blur national, racial, and color lines:* *The so-called Afro-Uruguayans were transported in slave ships from West Africa to the Americas. Africa is a continent which has fifty-three (53) countries and was most likely named after a Phoenician prefix and Latin suffix, speaking the Spanish and Creole language, and classifying their national and racial identity from a Guarani word.*

**Uruguay**: Uruguay" is a Guaraní word meaning "river of shellfish," or "river from which the uru birds come."

BYWORD

leadership, courage, resilience, faith, and contributions towards making the United States of America great. Lucy Terry (1746) and Phyllis Wheatley (1773) were notable Israelite women and authors who sought to shed light on our greatness among the heathen American sons of Japheth. The David Walker Appeal (1785) demanded so-called Negro slaves to rise up and revolt against their oppressors. Later, Nat Turner's revolt also known as the Southampton Insurrection put Walker's and others' words to the test. Following the revolt, the severity of slavery and slave laws became worse, primarily in Georgia and the Carolinas. In 1787, slavery was made illegal in Northwest Territory (1787). In 1793, Eli Whitney thought that by inventing the cotton gin, slavery would not be necessary. He was wrong; more slaves were put to work as the South attempted to industrialize it to compete with the North. In 1800, Gabriel Prosser led

a slave revolt (1800). In 1808, the U.S. Congress bans importation of slaves from Africa, claiming that such slaves (Geechies and Gullahs) were too difficult to handle and were not manageable as much as slaves who had succumbed psychologically to the twisted sons of the Gentile Caucasian's perverse lifestyles and ideologies in the United States.

The Missouri Compromise and Compromise of 1850 along with the Fugitive Slave Act further showed the evil of the American government as an anti-Semitic nation that continued to thrive off the lives of Israelite slaves and free denizens. On February 27, 1865, Delaney was commissioned as the U.S. Army's first black line field officer. *Frederick Douglass, Harriet Tubman, and Sojourner*

## ELDER MARK MAKABI

***Truth*** were key members in the freedoms of Israelites in the United States. Notable Israelites of the next generation were W.E.B. DuBois and Booker T. Washington. Notable events were the Pan-African movement from 1890 to 1919, and the possibility of returning to Africa beyond the establishment of the tumultuous Liberia.

African Americans fought in the First and Second World War separate from whites, then integrated during the Korean War and Viet Nam Wars and so on. The modern Civil Rights Movement under Dr. Martin Luther King, Medgar Evers, Rosa Parks and others, including the modern Black Nationalist Movement under Malcom X (El-Hajj Malik El-Shabazz), and later H. Rap Brown and Huey P. Newton of the Black Panther Party led up to our modern sense of "Blackness" in America and the election of President Barack Obama *(although he is of Hamitic/Kenyan descent and not an Israelite)*

**Historical Highlights***: Demark Vesey (1822), Nat Turner (1831), the Amistad revolt (1839), Frederick Douglas' newspaper (1846), the Wilmot Proviso introduce (1846),* **Harriet Tubman and the Underground Railroad** *(1849), the Compromise of 1850,* **Josiah Henson** *and Harriet Beecher Stowe's novel "Uncle Tom" (1852). The Kansas-Nebraska Act (1854), the Dred Scott Case (1857), John Brown's raid for freedom (1859), the Civil War (1861), Freedman Bureau, Abraham Lincoln assassinated, KKK formed in Tennessee* **led by an impostor Jew Nathan Bedford Forrest** *(1866), Juneteenth (1865), and the 13$^{th}$ Amendment ratified (1865), the Black Codes (1866), Reconstruction (1867), the 14$^{th}$ Amendment ratified (1868), Howard University Law School (1869), the 15$^{th}$ Amendment ratified (1870), Hiram Revels (U.S Senator of Mississippi, 1870-1871), Reconstruction ends (1877),* **Ida B. Wells (1862-1931),** *Booker T.*

# BYWORD

*Washington founds Tuskegee (1881), American Colonization Society (1882), Plessy V. Ferguson (1896), W.E.B DuBois founds the Niagara Movement, the precursor of the N.A.A.C.P. (1905), the NAACP (1909), Marcus Garvey founds the Universal Negro Improvement Association (1914), the Harlem Renaissances (1920s), the Scottsboro Trial (1931), Jackie Robinson (1947);* **side note**: *Although, I admire Jackie Robinson's courage and character to endure playing in a hostile arena, I do not celebrate the so-called Baseball integration because it was a sinister plan to break up the successful and popular Negro Baseball League.*

**Historical Highlights:** *The U.S. Armed forces integrated (1948), the Israelite fathers and mothers were the originators* 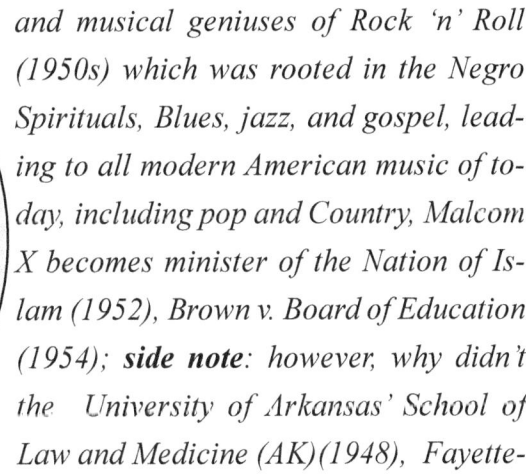 *and musical geniuses of Rock 'n' Roll (1950s) which was rooted in the Negro Spirituals, Blues, jazz, and gospel, leading to all modern American music of today, including pop and Country, Malcom X becomes minister of the Nation of Islam (1952), Brown v. Board of Education (1954);* **side note**: *however, why didn't the University of Arkansas' School of Law and Medicine (AK)(1948), Fayetteville and Charleston AK public schools (1954), and Hoxie Public School (AK) (1955) which integrated their schools without incident, previous to the Little Rock Nine (1957) receive national acknowledgements? Emmett Till (1955), Rosa Parks (1955), the Little Rock Nine (1957), The Student Nonviolent Committee Protest (1960), Freedom Riders (1961), James Meredith (1962), James L.*

## Elder Mark Makabi

*Farmer Jr., Dr. James F. Martin III, Dr. Martin L. King, Dr. Fred Shuttlesworth, Minister David Abernathy, March on Washington (1963), the 16th Street Church bombing in Birmingham, AL, (1963), Civil Rights Acts Signed (1964), James E. Chaney, Andrew Goodman, and Michael Schwerner, (1964), Dr. Martin L. King wins Noble Peace Prize and Sidney Poitier wins the Best Actor Oscar (1964), Civil Rights Act (1964), U.S. Congress passes Voting Right Act (1965), Huey Newton and Bobby Seale founded the Black Panther Party (1966), and Thurgood Marshall appointed to the Supreme Court Justice (1967).*

**Historical Highlight**: *Shirley Chisholm (1968), the Tuskegee syphilis experiment (1932-1972) the classic Roots TV mini-series (1977), Regents of University of California v. Bakke (affirmative action begins) (1978), Guion Bluford Jr.(1977-1979) Hip-Hop (1983), the race riots in south central Los Angeles, CA begin, following the Rodney King trial and four racist Caucasians police officers are acquitted, (1992), Colin Powell becomes the Secretary of State (2001**), the Bamboozled movie (2002**), Grutter v. Bollinger (2003), Condoleezza Rice (2005), Parents v. Seattle and Meredith v. Jefferson (2006). Although he is called African-American, President Barack Obama is a Hamite (African) and not an Israelite (2008-2016).* **Is the alleged placement of our Israelite mother Harriett Tubman on the American twenty dollar bill a paradox?**

**Origin of the name**: America was named by two Germans Martin Waldseemuller and/or Matthias Ringmann after an Italian explorer, Amerigo Vespucci. **"Afar"** Phoenician word and **"Ica" is Latin "Africa"**. In December 1988, presidential candidate and iconic leader, Jesse Jackson used the term "African-American" at a news conference in Chicago versus the somewhat archaic term Afro-American.

**Geography**: North America. United States of America

**Demographics**: An estimate of 13% or 25 million of the populations are Israelites *(the descendant of slaves)*. However, many so-called "mixed" or bi-racial people identify with their supposed European, Native American, or so-called Latino heritage. The so-called African Americans are actually more prominent in society in population than many Americans are led to believe.

***Clarifying the blur national, racial, and color lines***: *The so-called African-Americans were transported in slave ships from West Africa to the Americas. Africa is a continent which has fifty-three (53) countries and was most likely named after a Phoenician prefix and Latin suffix, speaking the English language, and classifying their national and racial identity after a continent with a Hamitic and Latinized origin and the name of an Italian explorer that was named by Germans.*

**African**: Afar" is Phoenician (*Sidon*) and "Ica" is Latin "Africa"

**American:** Ringmann or Waldseemuller (*Germans*) named America after an Italian explorer, **Amerigo Vespucci.** "Additional historical sources suggest that America was named after an Indian tribe in South America called "Americu" which means flying serpent"

**Who's Your Father?** Who named Israelite's African-Americans?

**In regards to your national identity, African-American is a byword:** Ridicule

**Byword guides us back to our nation:**
    Biblical nation of Israel
    Race: Semitic

## ELDER MARK MAKABI

Color of skin: Seven shades of brown
Language: Hebrew
Motherland: Jerusalem, Israel

## GUYANESE

**Historical Highlight:** Before the Dutch arrived to Guyana the original inhabitants were the Arawak and so-called Carib Amerindians. In 1616, the Dutch established the first European settlement in Guyana with the intentions of trading. The agriculture and economy increased as the Israelites slaves became an essential element in the development and prosperity of the colony. **From 1763 to 1764,** the brutality of slavery led to the famous Israelite slave revolt known as the ***"Berbice Slave Rebellion".*** The revolt was led by the great Israelite general named ***"Coffy the Great."*** The revolt began on a plantation called ***"Magdalenenburg"*** where Israelites killed, plundered, and burned the Europeans and their houses. "Coffy the Great" was considered a house slave who organized over 3000 Israelites as a fighting force. Unfortunately, during the rebellion, many mulattos sided with the Europeans. "Coffy the Great", whose revolt became the foundation for revolution, is an Israelite national hero that understood there's a time to kill.

**Origin of the name:** Derives from the indigenous people in reference to the large number of rivers in their land.

**Geography:** South America.

**Demographics:** An estimate of 42.6% of the population are Israelites *(descendant of slaves).*

***Clarifying the blur national, racial, and color lines:*** *The so-called Guyanese were transported in slave ships from West Africa to the Americas. Africa is a continent which has fifty-three (53) coun-*

## BYWORD

*tries and was most likely named after a Phoenician prefix (Afar) and Latin suffix (ica), speaking the English and Guyanese Creole languages, and classifying their national and racial identity after the land that derives from the indigenous inhabitants.*

**Guyana:** "large rivers" or "land of many rivers".

**Who's Your Father?** Who named Israelite's Guyanese?

**In regards to your national identity, Guyanese is a byword:** Mockery

**Byword guides us back to our nation:**
> Biblical nation of Israel
> Race: Semitic
> Pigmentation: Seven shades of blackness
> Language: Hebrew
> Homeland: Jerusalem, Israel

### TRINIDADIANS

**Historical Highlight**: Throughout the 1500s, the first Israelites were imported to cultivate tobacco, cocoa and the sugar. The Spanish King, José de Gálvez, (1783) decreed the *"Cédula de Población"* which granted free lands to Roman Catholic Christians of all European nations that brought their Israelite captives to Trinidad and swore allegiance to the Spanish king. The French, the Courlanders (Polish-Lithuanians), the Scottish, Irish, Germans, Italians, and English arrived by 1762 and treated the Israelite slaves with no dignity as they smuggled the Israelites around the world like commodities. Woe unto them! We honor and remember our scholar Dr. Tony Martin.

**Origin of the name**: Christopher Columbus named this Island in honor of the so-called "Trinity" (1498).

**Israelites Book of the Covenant**: There is no doctrine of the trinity, which is three gods. **Mark 12:29,** "And Jesus answered him, The first of all the commandments is, **Hear, O Israel; The Lord our God is one Lord:** The doctrine of the trinity was created during the First and Second Councils of Nicaea, which sought to appease the polytheistic nature of pagan legal and religious authorities among the Greeks and Romans who did not understand how to reconcile the Father, Son, and Holy Spirit being one.

**Geography**: Caribbean.

**Demographics**: An estimate of 58% of the population are Israelites *(descendant of slaves including Tobago).*

*Clarifying the blur national, racial, and color lines:* *The so-called Trinidadians were transported in slave ships from West Africa to the Americas. Africa is a continent which has fifty-three (53) countries and was most likely named after a Phoenician prefix (Afar) and Latin suffix (ica), speaking the English language, and classifying their national and racial identity after the name of the island that an Italian named after a bogus doctrine invented by the Roman Catholics.*

**Trinidad:** Trinity

**Who's Your Father?** Who named Israelite's Trinidadians?

**In regards to your national identity, Trinidadian is a byword:** Ridicule

**Byword guides us back to our nation:**
    Biblical nation of Israel
    Race: Semitic
    Color of skin: Seven shades of brown
    Language: Hebrew
    Motherland: Jerusalem, Israel

# BYWORD

## QUILOMOBOS

**Historical Highlight**: The Quilomobos where escaped, self-emancipated Israelite captives that established their own communities called palenques. The Quilomobos established a structure of resistance against their Portuguese oppressors. ***Zumbi dos Palmares*** was a great Israelite general that led his people to freedom. He was a man who was born free in the Palmares region which is known today as *"Alagoas State"* of Brazil, established in 1655. In addition, Zumbi was an extraordinary military genius, well organized, and developed a self-supporting community. He had a major role as an icon of freedom in the Israelite slave résistance for over 100 years. Zumbi the Great was beheaded in November 1695 by the Portuguese. Nevertheless, the organization called ***Zumbi +10*** continues to fight against racism in honor of Brazil's national Israelite hero Zumbi. Zumbi +10 was established on November 29, 2005 in Brazil.

**Origin of the name**: Quilomobo derives from Kilombo which is a Bantu word for encampment. Bantu is native language spoken in modern day Angola.

**Geography**: Brazil, South America

**Demographics**: An estimate of 44.7% of the population are Israelites *(descendant of slaves)*.

***Clarifying the blur national, racial, and color lines****: The so-called Quilomobos were transported in slave ships from West Africa to the Americas. Africa is a continent which has fifty-three (53) countries and was most likely named after a Phoenician prefix and Latin suffix, speaking the Portuguese language and related patois dialects, and classifying their national and racial identity from a name that derives from the Bantu language of Angola.*

**Quilomobos:** Encampment runaway slave resistance, a place of refuge.

**Who's Your Father?** Who named Israelite's Quilomobos?

**In regards to your national identity, Quilomobo is a byword:** Mockery

**Byword guides us back to our nation:**
    Biblical nation of Israel
    Race: Semitic
    Pigmentation: Seven shades of blackness
    Language: Hebrew
    Homeland: Jerusalem, Israel

## GULLAH/ GEECHEE

**Historical Highlight:** The Gullahs/Geehees are known for preserving more of their Israelite heritage than any other enslaved Israelites in the Americas. It is believed the Gullah derived from what is now Sierra Leone. In 1750, the British heathens, Henry Laurens and Richard Oswald opened a slave castle called "Bunce Island" on Sierra Leon River. The Gullahs were skilled agriculturalists, artisans, scientists, and engineers. They cultivated a multimillion-dollar rice industry in North America along the Atlantic coasts of North Carolina, South Carolina, Georgia, and Florida.

**Origins of the name:** There are several opinions concerning the origin of the names. The consensus among historical scholars is that "Gullah" derives from "Guale" the name the Spanish called the South Carolina and Georgia coastal region after a Native American tribe. Geechee comes from the "Ogeechee River" from the Creek Indian phrase "river of the Uchees (Yuchi) people"..

# BYWORD

**Geography**: North America: North Carolina, South Carolina, Georgia, and Florida.

**Demographics**: An estimate of nearly 250,000 Israelites *(the descendants of slaves).*

***Clarifying the blur national, racial, and color lines***: *The so-called Gullah/Geechee were transported in slave ships from West Africa to America. Africa is a continent which has fifty-three (53) countries and was most likely named after a Phoenician prefix and Latin suffix, speaking an English-based Creole language, and classifying their national and racial identity from a Spanish term that was most likely named after an Indian tribe and a river which derives from an Amerindian word for a river and a native people.*

**Gullah:** Spanish name after an Indian tribe, the Gaule.

**Geechee:** Named after a river from a Creek Indian word "Uchee" or "Yuchi".

**Who's Your Father?** Who named Israelite's "Gullah/Geechee"?

**In regards to your national identity, Gullah/ Geechee is a byword:** Ridicule

**Byword guides us back to our nation:**
    Biblical nation of Israel
    Race: Semitic
    Color of skin: Seven shades of brown
    Language: Hebrew
    Motherland: Jerusalem, Israel

## BYWORD UP!

*Prophet, what's your name?* **Abraham.** *What's your nationality?*

## Elder Mark Makabi

*Hebrew. The fame of your **name** is that you're the father of faith, the man in which all nations would be blessed, Abraham, this may sound **absurd** but I heard your Israelite descendants would become a **byword**;*

*Beautiful sister, what is your name? **Sarah.** What's your nationality? **Hebrew.** The fame of your **name** is that you're the mother of the "Children of the Covenant"; however, I heard through the grapevine, for the daughters of the covenant, their roles would be **blurred**, their motherhood **slurred**, their masculinity **spurred**, their femininity **deterred**, their existence **disturbed**,*

*Brother, what's your name? **Isaac.** What's your nationality? **Hebrew.** The fame of your **name** is that you're the greatest and only son of Abraham, the child of the covenant; Brother Isaac, the prophecy of the **word** is that your Israelite descendants will become a **proverb**,*

*Brother, what's your name? **Jacob.** What's your nationality? **Hebrew.** The fame of your **name** is that the most High changed your name to **Israel,** the father of the twelve tribes, the chosen nation that would be blessed above all people; but, **Israel** is **obscured,** your children have become a **proverb,** their nationality a **slur**; their identity a **blur**,*

*Brown sugars, what are your names? **Rachel, Leah, Zilpah, and Bilhah;** what's your nationality? We're **Hebrews;** the fame of your **names** is that you are the women who build up the nation of Israel. But it's sad to report in the 21$^{st}$ century most of your daughters have **morally erred** and become **abortion baby murderers**.*

# BYWORD

*Brother, what's your name?* **Joseph.** *What's your nationality?* **An Israelite,** *the fame of your* **name** *is that you were sold into slavery in Egypt, interpreted Pharaoh's dream, and became the Governor of Egypt, from a slave to a master; your Israelite descendants would return to Egypt, again in ships and with yokes around their necks; I* **overheard** *they would be reduce to becoming a* **by-word-up;**

*Brother man, what's your name?* **Moses.** *What's your nationality?* **An Israelite** *from the* **tribe of Levi.** *The fame of your* **name** *is* **"Let my people go!"** *You lead Israel out of Egypt, the house of bondage, where the Children of Israel walked through the Red Sea on dry ground. Moses you gave the prophetic* **word** *that the* **Israelites** *would* **disobey,** *and called out of their name because from the God of Abraham, they* **turned away;**

*Brothers, what are your names?* **The Maccabees.** *What's your nationality?*

**Israelites.** *The fame of your* **names** *is that you brothers were* **valiant warriors,** *defended the honor of your nation of Israel, defeated the heathen Greeks, and restored Israel's independence, from super men to fags and sissies how did this wicked phenomenon occur?*

*Virtuous sister, what's your name?* **Esther.** *What's your nationality?* **An Israelite.** *The fame of your* **name** *is that you became* **Queen** *during the reign of Ahasuerus, a sister who was promoted to* **prestige,** *but remained humble and did not forget her people's* **needs,** *a beautiful sister who honors her ancestors by being obedient to* her uncle Mordecai and saved her people from being slaughtered; **From Esther to Jezebel**, the **reverse effect**, many of your sisters have become the **devil's silhouette**, A sister like Esther is **preferred** but many of her sisters have become **Jezebel's slur;**

Brother, what's your name? **King David.** What's your nationality? **An Israelite**. The fame of your **name** is that you're a man after God's own heart, the original superman, the man who slew Goliath, who would believe your descendants would adopt the spirit of the heathens Gentiles, Gog and Magog, and go from being lions to dogs?

Brother, what's your name? **King Solomon**. What's your nationality? **An Israelite**. The fame of your **name** is all about your wisdom; from wisdom to buffoonery many of your descendants seem to **prefer** and **concur with** the **spirit** of minstrel **bywords?**

My brother, what's your name? **Jesus of Nazareth.** What's your nationality? **An Israelite** from the **tribe of Judah,** the true Jew, the brother with the good, wooly, and nappy hair, the fame of your **name** is great, you're the Christ, the sacrificial Lamb for the Nation of Israel, the first fruit of the resurrection, King of Kings and Lord of Lords, proclaiming the **Negroes** are the blood descendants of **Jesus Christ of Nazareth to the world is absurd; look at all those** Negroes! They're calling themselves **bywords;**

Brother, what's your name? **Paul,** what's your nationality? **An Israelite** from the **tribe of Benjamin,** the fame of your **name** is you persecuted Israelites because you believed they were changing the laws, your name was changed from Saul to Paul, and your mission

## BYWORD

*was to teach the pagan Gentiles, Europeans, the doctrine of Israel, you recorded your nationality in **Romans 11:1**, your kinsmen, your **brethren** written about in the book of **Deuteronomy 28:37**.*

# CHAPTER 6
# THE BYWORD WAS MADE FLESH!
## *"Unmasking the Face of Minstrelsy"*

### Psalm 23

> "The Lord is my shepherd; I shall not want. He maketh me to lie down in green pastures: he leadeth me beside the still waters. He restoreth my soul: he leadeth me in the paths of righteousness for his name's sake. Yea, though I walk through the valley of the shadow of death, I will fear no evil: for thou art with me; thy rod and thy staff they comfort me. Thou preparest a table before me in the presence of mine enemies: thou anointest my head with oil; my cup runneth over. Surely goodness and mercy shall follow me all the days of my life: and I will dwell in the house of the Lord forever."

Psalm 23 is the greatest poetic expression that was ever produced since the beginning of time. Psalm 23 is an extraordinary, artistic expression of devotion that transcends time, cultures, races, sexes, generations, religions, and languages. It is an expression of creative genius, imagination, norms, and reflections, values, experiences, aspirations, and ideals of the Israelites (descendants of slaves in the Americas). King David was an Israelite, the author, the poet, and the songwriter of Psalm 23. His Psalm exceeded the popularity of Michael Jackson, Smokey Robinson, Curtis Mayfield, Louis Armstrong, Ben Blackwell, Charlie Parker, Smokey Robinson, The Supremes, Tina Turner, Al Green, Little Richard, John Coltrane, Billie Holiday, Lauryn Hill, Temptations, Jackie Wilson, Drake, Biggie Smalls, Nas, Kendrick Lamar, KRS-One, DMX, Duke Ellington, Dizzy Gillespie, Ella Fitzgerals, Chuck D, Common, Miles Davis, Sade, Art Tatum, Mahalia Jackson, Andrea Crouch, Ray Charles, James Brown, Aretha Franklin, Marvin Gaye, Whitney Houston, Bob Marley, Stevie Wonder, Prince, Rick James, Jimi Hendrix, The Temptations, Beyoncé, B.B. King, Miles Davis, Tupac, Jay-Z the Beatles, Elvis Presley, Garth Brooks, Frank Sinatra, Britney Spears, Barbra Streisand, and the Rolling Stones combined.

King David did not have a record or publishing deal with Sony, Grand Hustle, RCA, and Aftermath, a Hollywood movie studio, or Warner Brothers. King David did not have investors in the marketing, promoting, and distribution of Psalm 23 music videos, digital recordings, images, movies, books, merchandising, or international tours. The inspiration of Psalm 23 was not driven by vanity, fame, fortune, greed, pride, lust, power, betrayal, misuse, corruption, being politically correct, peer pressure, influences of the mass media or politics, values, and/or morals that were contrary to his Israelite heritage.

Psalm 23 creatively reflects our cultural values, social values, norms, imaginations, artistic genius, folkways, mores, taboos, pride, family values, spirituality, aspirations, ideals, and established our national tone of our Israelite nation. Our arts were governed or driven by our faith which we expressed as our **"Rock"**. This **"Rock"** reinforces our Israelite-Biblical values whereas the nature of our cultural and artistic expression historically has been celebrated as our *"national treasures"*. These natural treasures were not governed by vanity, politics, lobbyists, the national endowment of the arts, a curriculum, or measured by box-office sales. The artist expression of Israel reflects the wisdom of its people, the understanding of advanced concepts of the nature, righteousness, and of the human soul.

The Israelites had advanced knowledge of the nature of the creative arts and how it influence and promoted righteousness, human development, and development in the disciplines of science, mathematics, medicine, technology, anatomy, biology, law, psychology, engineering and many more. For example, the core theory of evolution and natural selection supports creation in that evolution is a **"process"** and a process involves **creation; creation involves thought.** Therefore, anything that is created has a creator. Additionally, the core theory of evolution involves **"change"** or **"to make"** and **"to make"** is the same as to **create**. The scientific community should consider the value of the creative arts and the contributions they have made to science. Our creative arts reflected our high-concept of our self-value, relevance, humanity, and natural rhythm of creation that would be the envy of all nations, and bless the Israelites above all nations including nations with the same pigmentation *(i.e. Africans, Ancient Egyptians, Nubians Ethiopians, etc.)*.

# BYWORD

The rhythm of the Biblical nation of Israel expresses the symmetrical nature of movement of creation that was intended to edify the asymmetrical nations and reveal the difference between what is regular and irregular. Thus, the rhythm of Israel produces perfect harmonious vibrations and provides a holistic method to correct the nature of irregularity of the asymmetrical nations so that they can be in harmony with the nature of creation. **The rhythm of Israel "ROCKS" like poetry in motion and has produced the greatest music in history that the rhythm-less nations have envied and aspired to imitate** to the level in which the rhythm-less *(i.e. Europeans)* such as: *Stephen Foster, Thomas "Daddy" Rice, Benny Goodman, George Gershwin, Irving Berlin, Elvis Presley, Hank Williams, Jeff Beck, Tom Jones, The Beatles, the Bee-Gees, KC & The Sunshine Band, The Rolling Stones, especially Mick Jagger, Janis Joplin, Eminem, Iggy Azaela, and many other American European-Caucasians have stolen, emulated, and like parasites- profited from the rhythm of the Israelites.*

*The American institution of racism (i.e. the Rolling Stone Magazine) continues to express their lies that Elvis Presley, originally a social outcast among other whites because he was poor and grew up among Blacks and who idolized and learned from his master* **Arthur "Big Boy" Crudup** *is hailed as the so-called King of Rock and Roll; however, the historical account of Elvis Presley's original reception by the majority of whites in the South and North was synonymous with the* **so-called (white) citizens' councils in the South's reaction… calling Elvis Presley's music… "nigger music"**

Rolling Stone magazine is an example of the institution of racism that continues to promote "so-called white supremacy "in their

## ELDER MARK MAKABI

endeavor to rewrite our **great Israelite Rock and Roll history** by placing **Caucasians as the face of rock and roll music.** Furthermore, Billboard, the Grammys, American Music Awards, Country Music Awards, American Idol, and the American media is currently attempting to place Iggy Azaela and Eminem as the face of our Israelite Hip-Hop and Robin Thicke as the face of our "soul" music/Rhythm & Blues; however an imitator can never be the originator, and a graft is not the root.

Our remarkable rhythm produced artistic genius such as **Lewis Latimer**, **Stevie Wonder**, Anthony J. "Satchmo" McNeil, **Johnnie Cochran**, Richard Pryor, **Michael Jordan**, Jelly Roll Morton, **Tee Tot Payne**, Robert Johnson, **Spike Lee**, Paul Mooney, **Michael Jackson**, Jessie Owens, **Bob Marley**, Tiger Woods, **Louis Armstrong**, Pele, **Sammy Davis Jr**, Jim Brown(Football), **Malcom X**, Maya Angelou, **Tupac**, Willie Mays, **Muhammad Ali**, Muddy Waters, **Dick Gregory**, Art Tatum, **John Coltrane**, Joe "Brown Bomber" Louis, **Mahalia Jackson**, Lena Horne, **William Henry Lane**, Gordon Parks, **Aretha Franklin**, Billie Holliday, James Brown, **Denzel Washington,** Jacob Lawrence, **Bill Cosby**, Elder Ben Melech, Kenneth "Babyface" Edmonds, **Oscar Micheaux,** Henry Ossawa Tanner, **Bill "Bojangles" Robison**, Saint Ernestine, **Cornel West**, Gil Scott Heron, **Elder Shadrock**, Miles Davis, **Curtis Mayfield**, Sylverster "Sly" Stone, **Bob Marley**, Eddie Murphy, Ronald Isley, Marvelous Marvin Hagler, William "Bootsy" Collins, **Sugar Ray Robinson**, Whitney Houston, **Avery W. McNeil**, O.J. Simpson,

# BYWORD

***Sister Souljah***, *Public Enemy,* ***Isaac Hayes,*** ***KRS One****, Bill Duke,* ***Jimi Hendrix,*** *George Clinton,* ***Oscar L. McNeil,*** *Forest Whitaker,* ***Ray Charles***, ***Nate King Cole****,* ***Paul Robeson****, Andre Crouch,* ***Nicholas Brothers****, Prince, Dave Chappelle,* ***Louis Jordan****, Minister Ortez Vandross,* ***Fats Domino****, Bo Diddley, , Chuck Berry,* ***B.B. King,*** *Little Richard,* ***Billy Blanks****, Dr. James F. Martin III,* ***Rossetta Tharpe****, Jim "Black Belt "Kelly,* ***Elder Clement****, Victor Moore,* ***Dr. Martin Luther King,*** *James L Farmer,* ***Marcus Garvey****, Willie Mae "Big Mama" Thorton and many more…*

The rhythm of Israel *(descendant of slaves)* is an innate quality that is not limited to our musical prowess; rather, the rhythm sense of balance is expressed in the flow of our *vernacular, cuisine, intellect, colloquialisms, gestures, athleticism, charisma, dancing, stride, salutations, body language, romance, flamboyance, sexual prowess, spatial sense, cadence in our speech, learning style, imaginations, theatrical flow, oratorical flow, resilience, faith, dialects, tone, festivities, and overall culture.*

The rhythm Israel exudes is a blessing; it is the Creator's archetype to enlighten the rhythm-less nations to recognize and align themselves with the flow of creation. However, the horrendous effects of the Israelites forsaking their covenant, seduced, and defiling their God-given-rhythm led to the rhythm-less nations owning, controlling, and profiting from the God of Israel's rhythm, among the many blessings he bestowed upon his beloved, chosen people.

## "FLOETIC SOUL"

*The nature of rhythm's spiritual expression moves with the harmony of the Creator's love for life, flowing with the rain drops rhythmic spices, expressing the rhythmic vibes of the Israelites melodic soul, which divides the day from the night, syncopates darkness' void with the eternal light, ferments wine's swing, fine-tunes the joyful sounds of the mountains silhouettes, improvises the cool-Jazz-breeze, whistles the lilies of the valley' pitch, composes the landscapes lyrics, sings the songs of the stars, dances to the melody of the moonlight, plays the scales of the seasons, expresses the voice of the heavens, orchestrates the choir of the clouds, composes the 7th note rest, harmonizes in 12 keys, humming the lovers' duet, the male and female perfect pitch in the Key of Life natural fit, and rocks the sunrise soul to sunsets rest...*

Moreover, the Israelites are the creators and originators of Rock music and was **rocking and rolling** since the time of their Exodus in 1446 B.C.

**PSALM 95:1** - *"O come, let us SING unto the LORD: LET US MAKE A JOYFUL NOISE TO THE ROCK OF OUR SALVATION."*

Furthermore, one of the first recorded Rock song was created and written by an Israelite named **Moses** as express in the Israelite Book of the Covenant.

**DEUTERONOMY 32:4** - "He is the **ROCK,** his work is perfect: for all his ways are judgment: a God of truth and without iniquity, just and right is he."

**DEUTERONOMY 32:44** - *"And **Moses** came and spake all the words of this **SONG** in the ears of the people, he, and Hoshea the son of Nun."*

## BYWORD

The nature of our creative artistic and rhythmical genius created and produced **Rock & Roll music, vernacular, and culture which originally reflected our national faith (e.g. He is the ROCK).** However, the Biblical nation of Israel had a choice to be free to serve in the rhythm of creation or to be slaves to the rhythmless nations in captivity. Thus, the Israelite (Biblical) holocaust of slavery would be a deplorable condition that would lead to the rise of the minstrels and how the descendant of slaves would fulfill the Biblical prophecy of how a nation would become the **byword** that was made flesh among the heathens as a result of forsaking their covenant with the Lord.

> **PSALM 44:14**
> *"You have made us a byword among the nations;*
> *the peoples shake their heads at us."*

One of the most horrific effects of slavery was how the ***sons of Esau** (e.g. **Edomites are the imposters calling themselves Jew-ish or Israeli) and the Gentile sons of Japheth (European-Caucasians)*** denied the slaves of their human rights by denying *them* the knowledge of self and replacing that knowledge with corrupt information that dehumanized them to a status of a Byword or a nonperson. This conspiracy was devised, developed, and disseminated through the institutions of arts and entertainment in the format of the **American White-Trash Minstrels**. Nevertheless, historically the "minstrel" was an European tradition dating back to the ***" European Dark Ages"*** (500-1500 AD) which refers to a period of time of backwardness, epidemic diseases, the "Bubonic" plague, feudalism, serfdom, the Crusades, famine, and when the **Gentile sons of Japheth (Europeans)** were in intellectual darkness and barbarity.

Minstrels means *"servant," "little servant" and/or "entertaining servant" "good-for-nothing"*, and *"rogue"* akin to the modern *"thug"* term celebrated by misguided Israelite *(so-called African-Americans)* youth in America. So-called European nobles would often employ these minstrel servants for their household amusement. Moreover, the artistic talent of minstrels was considered average compared to the *"Troubadours"* and during the Dark Ages many people perceived the minstrels as buffoons beneath a court jester also referred to as "the fool". There were wandering minstrels that would wander from house to house to earn a silver penny by performing their minstrel act such as a comedic buffoonery, playing a lute, chanting songs, reciting poems, dancing, mythical and folklore storytelling, juggling, fire eating, acrobatics, and magic- basically a circus or carnival act. The fictional character **"Alan-A-Dale"** who joined the Robin Hood's gang as a famous minstrel.

The Gentile sons of Japheth (Europeans) transported their minstrel traditions across the seas to America where they stole, appropriated, redefined, rewrote, and corrupted the creative artistic genius, musicianship, vernacular, rhythm, dance, music, physical features, cultural expressions, and racial identity of the *Hebrew-Israelite slaves* and assimilated their minstrel tradition to produce **"American White-trash minstrel"** arts and entertainment **shows**. These shows began as early as the 1830s. The American White-trash Minstrels reflected the inhumane values of the sons of Esau and the sons of Japheth which is primarily driven by a conniving and immoral disposition that promoted a human's worth is based on material possessions which established the national tone of racism in the Americas.

The creative artistic expression of the Israelites reflected the value of the soul of humanity, driven by their sacred disposition that human worth is based on the righteous and just treatment of human beings from which the expression ***soul music*** derived- expressions of the value all people can relate to that lies in our perception of not individuality but the collective soul that is the essence of the Creator in all people of Earth. The most High is the author of the arts and reigns supreme as the greatest creative artist; in the beginning, **He CREATED the heavens, the earth**, and established the nature of the creative arts which reflected in the beauty, perfection, and balance of his artistic expression. This is seen in the *clouds, flowers, trees, seas, gold, gardens, fruits, rocks, herbs, gems, mountains, rivers, valleys, seasons, sun, diamonds, moon, stars, day, night, insects, waterfalls, animals, rainbow, grass, snow, rain, men, women, and children.* Thus, the creative artist has the opportunity to learn from the Creator the natural purpose of their aesthetic capability by observing nature. Nature is the greatest example of God's glory reflected in art in all six (6) senses; this allows artists to discover and develop their process of deciding how they will express their gifts from the Almighty.

The American White-trash minstrel performers blurred the color lines in their process to corrupt and redefine racial identity as a color, and as a result, they contaminated the artistic and cultural expressions of the Israelites in the ignorant racists' attempt to interpret Israelites gifts from God. Moreover, history suggest that the sons of Esau (Jewish) and the sons of Japheth (Caucasians) have a natural aptitude for corrupting nature's original order *(e.g. the abomination of so-called homosexual marriage)*. The American White-trash minstrels corrupted our natural melanin pigmentation by redefining an invalid racial classification across the color lines of black and white *(e.g. color does not determine race, ethnicity, or national identity); this blurred* the lines between race and color. Thus, the Caucasian American premise of defining "Blackness" pertaining to race is absurd.

The American White-trash minstrel shows created and displayed obscene and exaggerated images of our natural physical traits and cultural expressions to degrade our *natural vernacular flow* by developing the pejorative characters of racists' interpretations of Israelite beauty, strength, and cunning. The **"Coon" caricature** speaks in malapropisms. Our *natural chic* was used to create the image of the **"Pimp"**. Our *natural rhythm* was used to create the tap-dancing **"Buffoon"**. Our women's *natural assertiveness* was used to create the **"Boisterous Mammy" and "Saffire"**. Our **masculine prowess was used** to create the **"Buck, Brute, or Thug" caricature or the "oversexed Mandingo" caricature (i.e. D.W. Griffith's Birth of a Nation, 1915)**. These caricatures blurred the lines between our natural cultural expressions and minstrel stereotypes to invoke feelings that the natural artistic and cultural expressions of the Israelites was unnatural.

The American White-Trash Minstrels shows would display our natural **wooly hair, broad nose, and full-lips** and present them through the media as a **"Buckwheat" or "Pickaninny" caricature** to produce feelings that our wooly hair, full-lips, and broad nose was ugly and unnatural. This was and remains an attempt to blur the lines between natural self-love and unnatural self-hate for our natural wooly hair, full-lips, and broad nose (e.g. What is good hair?). The **Uncle Tom** caricature of being a spineless house negro and race traitor was a character assassination of Josiah Henson; this caricature came from the American minstrels not from the original characterization displayed in *Uncle Tom's Cabin* by Harriet Beecher Stowe's and Josiah Henson (1852).

Josiah Henson (1789-1883) was a brilliant leader, abolitionist, publisher, lecture, co-author, Underground Railroad conductor, founder of "Dresden Ontario," a city for runaway slaves, and was honored and featured on a Canadian stamp. America White-trash minstrels and the children's book **"Little Black Sambo"** by Helen Bannerman (1899) redefined, recreated, corrupted, and popularized the **Sambo** caricature of a dysfunctional, docile, and childish personality from its original noble and common name of the slaves meaning **"son or second son" among the Fulbe, Foulah, and Fulani people.** History suggests that the term **"coon"** derived from the Portuguese **"barracoos"** (meaning hut or enclosure for slaves, captives, and criminals) **or "raccoon."** The barracoos was where the minstrels were housed and exploited like "little animals" and created the **"zip coon" or "coon"** image.

Hollywood's movie premiere of **"King Kong" (1933) reflects the King Kong Kit (KKK) version of the Willie Lynch (1712) letter** and "Birth of a Nation" (1915), and how **thugs** dehumanized and criminalized their victims to justify their criminal behavior. These are primary examples of how using the media is a means to propagate psychological lynching of the Israelites in America and to blur the lines between justice and injustice. The movie plot highlights King Kong's sexual interest in a blonde-headed, white woman; the **European thugs'** illegal invasion, capture, and removal of King Kong from his natural habitat into the land of his captivity symbolizes attempts to colonize the lands of a real King, which represents the Black kings and queens and their sovereignty in Africa. From that point, the American media proceeded to place the Israelite in a state of perpetual thuggery and murder the concept of the "King", emasculating and dehumanizing "Black men" in effigy through imagery.

The impact of the American White-trash minstrels blurring the lines between color and race, black and white, the truth and lies may continue to persist with the children of slavery in their feelings of uncertainty when viewing, embracing versus denouncing, or supporting images and behavioral traits of themselves. **Spike Lee's classic movie,** ***Bamboozled,*** artistically demonstrated the social, racial, psychological, spiritual, color and racial fallout of the blurred lines. However, what were American White-trash minstrels? It was a psychological reflection, acknowledgement, and racist response by Caucasians concerning melanin, physical, sexual, rhythmical, moral, civil, artistic, and cultural deficiencies, the recognition of the superior rhythmical personas and artistic geniuses of the Israelites in America, and the fulfillment of the Biblical prophecy of how the Biblical nation of Israel would be reduced to becoming a Byword in the flesh.

For example, **Thomas "Daddy" Rice (1808-1860)** recognized the superior artistic genius and rhythmical persona of the Israelite slaves. Thomas "Daddy" Rice was an unsuccessful and inept actor that played a major role in the proliferation and popularization of the

BYWORD

minstrels, based on his observation of an Israelite slave singing and dancing to a song **"Jump Jim Crow."** Thomas "Daddy" Rice was a white-trash parasite who stole and imitated the song and dance routine of "Jump Jim Crow" and then proceeded to borrow the rags from a slave named **"Cuff"** in which he used during his debut performance of Jump Jim Crow. Jump Jim Crow became a smash hit and advanced Thomas "Daddy" Rice inept career. **Thomas "White-trash" Rice** received the justice he deserved when progressive paralysis short-cut his career and killed him at the age of 52. Nevertheless, the **honorable Fredrick Douglas** articulated his sentiments of the minstrels. **"Blackface performers are, "…the filthy scum of white society, who have stolen from us a complexion denied them by nature, in which to make money, and pander to the corrupt taste of their white fellow citizens."**

The honorable *Fredrick Douglas'* sentiments characterized the minstrel shows as the welfare program and affirmative action plan for America's **"White-trash"** society. Nevertheless, the psychological and social mask of the minstrels was the **"mocking"** which en-

abled the **American White-trash minstrels performers** to disguise their envy, admiration, and desire to emulate such superior innate qualities of being blessed with the nature's creation of melanin and to reconcile their desires and justify their delusional theory of so-called white supremacy.

The "American White-trash

162

minstrels" shows were not a cross-cultural collaboration, did not lead to widespread appreciation for the rich cultural expressions and the artistic genius of the Israelites in America, and it was not the route for the Israelites to succeed in the American entertainment industry. Charles Matthews did not invent the "Stump Speech". Stephen Foster and Charles Matthews songs were influenced by the music of the Israelites captives; therefore, American pop music is a mockery of Israelite music in America. The sons of Esau (Jewish) and the American sons of Japheth's (Caucasians) ownership and control of the minstrels served to define so-called "Blackness" nationally and internationally. Charles Matthew and Stephen Foster were racist White-trash thieves that observed, studied, and stole from the culture and artistic expression of the Israelites captives, denizens, and later citizens with the agenda to profit, considering the essence of minstrelsy and American White-trash buffoonery *in movies and productions such as Richard Pryor and Gene Wilder's (Jewish) Silver Streak, in which Gene Wilder performs in "burnt cork" in the bathroom scene (1976).*

There have always been models of intellectual brilliance among the descendant of Israelite slaves in the American conscious that dispelled America's White-trash, racist, minstrel images. For example, **Claud McKay** dispelled **Golliwog (a pickaninny-like character). Jessie Fauset** debunked the **Mammy, Lewis Latimer** dismissed the **Sambo. The Jubilee Singers** diminished **Stephen Foster's songs. Freedom's People** discredited **Amos & Andy. Micheaux (1920) "Within Our Gates"** challenged **"Birth of a Nation" (1915).** Jazz expressed our advanced Israelite culture, intellect, and artistic greatness to the entire world. The honorable **Paul Robeson's** academic, athleticism, singing, acting, and linguistic prowess discredited the **Coon.** *The honorable Robeson earned a law degree from Rutgers University and spoke eight (8) languages.*

The historical highlight of the American White-trash minstrel shows were between 1830-1890; however, these minstrels migrated to vaudeville, radio, film, and TV up into the 1960s. The ***American White-trash Minstrels*** *racist* shows were developed, organized, financed, controlled, and produced by the American Gentile sons of Japheth under the control of the Jewish Hollywood to reinforce America's racist disposition and hostility towards the true Israelites. In addition, the American White-trash minstrel shows played a historic role in blurring the lines between culture and stereotype, color and race, racist perceptions, and the circulation of their racist images that continue to influence popular entertainment today.

The historical consensus of the origins of the American Gentile sons of Japheth applying burnt cork to their pale faces begins with **Shakespeare's "Othello,"** the **"Padlock," "The Negro Boy" (Mr. Graupner), "** and **"Pot Pie Herbert"**. These led many racist White-trash minstrels parasites to follow such idiocy such as *Bob Farrell, George Nichols, Thomas "White-trash" Rice, P.T. Barnum, E. Byron Christy, Lew Dockstader, Daniel "Decatur" Emmett, Freeman Gosden, Charles Correll, J.H. Haverly, Judy Garland, Fred Astaire, Bing Cosby, the infamous Al Jolsen (a Russian Khazar impostor Jew) who sung "Mammy", Jimmy Durante, Eddie Cantor*, *and etc.* Moreover, these White-trash minstrels performed in **"DRAG"** *(e.g. The Only Leon, Tony Hart etc.)* to imitate, degrade, and circulate racist images of the so-called "black" woman as wenches and Jezebels. However, men and women who cross-dress *(e.g. cross-dressing* *or transvestitism is a form of physical, social, emotional, or racial insignias that is in binary opposition to his or her own)* are an abomination before the Lord and the Biblical nation of Israel.

> **DEUTERONOMY 22:5**
> **"The woman shall not wear that which pertaineth unto a man, neither shall a man put on a woman's garment: for all that do so are ABOMINATION unto the Lord thy God."**

The irony of the minstrel plot becomes peculiar when the descendants of slaves began to applied burnt cork to their black faces to **blur lines** between colorism, color and race, their natural cultural expressions and stereotypes, racism and prejudice, success and self-hatred, thus supporting their own oppression. For example, **Bert Williams and George Walker** were comedians; however, they defiled the honor of their Israelite heritage when they portrayed themselves as **"Two-Real Coons"** and were rewarded. **William "Master Juba" Lane** was a talented and prolific dancer who introduced **"Tap Dancing"** and the **Cakewalk"** to the American Gentile sons of Japheth and had the privilege of performing without burnt cork on his blackface. Thus, the national message of America and Hollywood to the descendant of slaves is "you can achieve wealth, fame, and some privileges if you conform to the racist and immoral values of White America." For example, *Hattie McDaniel won an Oscar award for the blur lines between the Mammy and her natural cultural expressions and degrading her own racial heritage.*

*Similar to the* Israelites like *Grandy, Douglas, and Brown*

# BYWORD

*(1839)* which led the worldwide abolition movement for the freedom of slavery, **Paul Robeson echoed their valor by stating, "The artist must elect to fight for freedom or for slavery."** Although, many descendant of slaves became part of the minstrel act, we should be careful, considerate, merciful, and sensitive in our assessments in judging them in their conditions of peonage, poverty, and oppression that racism produced in their decisions to choose among life, death, starvation, survival, and providing for their families. We must approach their example with the understanding that we reserve our cultural rights to decide and teach our children our Israelite standards for role models.

The imitation, bastardization, emasculation, and indignation of American entertainment concerning the Israelite in America created a distinct American identity that extended beyond the minstrels and vaudeville and into ole time radio, sit-coms, Amos & Andy, slapstick *(e.g. the Three Stooges)* stand-up comedy, variety shows such as *Jack Benny, Fred Allen, Laurel & Hardy, Abbott and Costello, I Love Lucy, Carol Burnette.* This knavery of entertainment influenced of the development of Hollywood's multi-billion dollar entertainment industry. With that in mind, Warner Brothers, Walt Disney, MGM, Merrie Melodies, Looney Tunes, NBC, CBS, RKO and others have played central roles in sustaining the racist Anti-Semitic national tone in the Americas in an attempt to further dehumanize and exploit the Biblical nation of Israel and its descendants of slaves in America.

## ELDER MARK MAKABI

Unfortunately, the level of self-hatred led many misguided individuals to seek acceptance from the enemies of the Israelites in America. This was and remains the hallmark of immoral values that so-called "Negros", stereotypically continue to promote themselves, being uneducated and rambunctious, hustlers, pimps, crooks, docile, deadbeat fathers, oversexed, brutes, and lazy buffoons. For instances shucking, jiving, grinning, and salutation of **"give me five on the black hand side"** is not minstrelsy, but perverted by the perspectives of *how the sons of Esau and the American sons of Japheth continue to blur the lines, attach immoral values to our images, cultural expressions, and perspectives in media, and the tradition of being a* **"lazy fool"** *like Steppin' Fetchit.* The American minstrels continue to **own the identity** of the descendant of slaves which reflects the legacy of minstrelsy and its ultimate insult rooted in slavery, being byword, perceived as a nonperson. **However, for the descendant of slaves to disown minstrelsy they must reclaim their Israelite identity.**

Moreover, the horrific effects of the minstrels blurring the lines and attaching immoral values to minstrelsy branded our natural God-given cultural and artistic expression. This can be observed in how the descendant of slaves internalized their self-hate *(e.g. how they feel when they see the mugshot images like William H. "Willie" Horton (1988) on TV, their reference to their nigger-self, when they conked and perm their good wooly hair, and their pursuit to conform to the American minstrel stigma and values in a vain attempt to be accepted in racist American society)*

The descendant of slaves must take responsibility for the role they play in their own self-destruction when they embrace and promote the American minstrel brand. For example, we can see the old process of the *King Kong Kit (KKK)* being used to marginalize the potent and brilliant art-form of Hip-hop *(e.g. Love and Hip-Hop).* The powerful record company executive create, finance, and promote the image of **"Sagging Pants, Gun Totting, Black Thugs"** in music videos. Later these same so-called Hip-hop **Black Thugs Gangstas** are demonized by *Fox's Bill O'Reilly, Sheriff David Clarke Jr., Larry Elder, Sean Hannity, Michael Savage, Rush Limbaugh, Glenn Beck, Mark Levine (impostor Jew), Ann Coulter, Sarah Palin, David Webb, Neal Boortz, Tammy Bruce, (She's perceived as a racist conservative so-called lesbian), Geraldo Rivera, Herman Cain, and Michelle Malkin to justify America's police terrorisms, murders, or lynching of so-called **menacing brute-thugs*** (i.e. D.W. Griffith's Birth of a Nation, 1915).

This is the process by which American corporate and Hollywood thugs attempt to change the image of their victims into criminals, then attack these victims, claiming they are a menace to society.

However, how often does a fox name Bill condemn the Jewish peoples record and movie executives, companies, and corporate America who sponsor, finance, promote, and distribute these menacing images and immoral messages to the American people? Furthermore, the descendant of Negro slaves who embrace and support these menacing images, FOX's *"Empire,"* **ABC's** *"Scandal,"* VH1 *"Love and Hip-Hop"* and similar programming **that degrades their Israelite heritage, cultural values, and holocaust of slavery** *(e.g. attempting to normalize homosexuality and abortion*) while hollering *"Black Lives Matter"* is hypocritical. Moreover, any attempt by the European sons of Japheth to impose homosexuality on the sons of Israel *(descendant of the so-called Negro slaves)* is a racist act of America's *so-called white supremacist ideology.*

> **II Peter 2:6**
> "And turning the cities of **Sodom and Gomorrha** into **ashes condemned them** with an overthrow, making them an **ensample** unto those that after should **live ungodly;**"

In addition, Hip-hop is a potent art form that was created and developed by the Israelites *(descendant of slaves)* as a social conscious media to elevate the nation emotionally, spiritually, socially, economically, and racially. However, Hip-hop is currently being branded as minstrelsy to blur the lines between the artistic phenomena of Hip-hop and minstrelsy of marginalization in American society. This evil generated by racist media has undermined Hip-hop's influence, greatness, and power. American minstrelsy blurred the lines between the children of Israel color and race and attached immoral values to their rich cultural genius. These immoral stereotypes were attached to the Israelite persona to humiliate, mock, and devalue the values and norms of the Israelites for a profit, "psychological and commercial slavery".

Once the **propaganda of** American minstrelsy **values** are recognized for the evil it is, the blur lines are cleared, and the truth of the American media system and its continuous attack upon Israelites in America is revealed. Therefore, the cultural and artistic expression of Hip-hop is not minstrelsy; however, it becomes minstrelsy when the artist expresses, supports, promotes, and conforms to perpetuating the **American white-trash minstrel values** that is contrary to the cultural values of the Israelite nation. Values are related to the norms of cultural standards of what is acceptable or unacceptable, important or unimportant, right or wrong, or good and evil. For example, cross dressing, so-called transsexual and transgender is an ***American white-trash minstrel value*** that is contrary to the values of the Biblical nation of Israel. **(Deuteronomy 22:5)** However, many sports figures, comedians, actors, singers, rappers, dancers, and celebrities have conformed to the immoral values of American minstrelsy of dressing in "drag" and are being financially rewarded for normalizing this immoral behavior to psychologically castrate and emasculate the black man (the Israelite man in America and abroad). **Woe unto the Judas Kissers!** Using the creative arts to glorify reckless **"sexual activity"** and **"killings"** is contrary to the Israelite values of the Ten Commandments such as **"thou shalt not kill"** and a number of Biblical norms.

The spiritual (Biblical) implications for the Israelites breaching their *Covenant of the Ten Commandments* would result in their identity being owned by the American media which began with the slaves codes and hijacked by the minstrels. This process of becoming a byword that was made flesh. **When Williams and Walker placed burnt-cork on their faces to be minstrels performers they became the living Coon which the American white-trash minstrels corrupted from the slaves and captives in the Barracoos, the living Sambo which the American White-trash minstrels corrupted from the Fulbe, the living "Tom" which the American White-**

## Elder Mark Makabi

**trash minstrels corrupted from the book Uncle Tom Cabin, the living Mammy which the American White-trash minstrels corrupted from the cultural assertiveness of our women, and the living Nigger which the American White-trash minstrels corrupted from the Latin word for black, "Niger".**

The American White-trash minstrels had power to give life unto the image of the minstrel beast *(i.e. Coon, Sambo, Thug, Nigger, Aunt Jemima, and Cesare Borgia)* through Hollywood's mass media. The role that the descendant of slaves have played to support their own self-destruction by worshiping the image of the minstrel beast is an abomination. There is a Jew-ish influences in Hollywood. The sinister role the Edomite *(Jewish)* sons of Esau played in proliferating American minstrelsy to corrupt the Israelite cultural arts and heritage is unnerving, *Al Jolson (1886-1950) is considered the father of American minstrelsy; however, his real name is Asa Yoelson. Asa Yoelson, Koster and Bials, the Ziegfeld Follies, and Hammerstein's Victoria Theater popularized the* **"Coon"** *which advanced the minstrel careers of Bert Williams and George Walker.* Moreover, the influence of American White-trash minstrels continues its racist traditions in modern day pop entertainment in America. For example, Jan Wenner *(An European impostor claiming to be a Jew)* is the co-founder of "Rolling Stone Magazine" which continues to place a Caucasian face on the Black man's Rock n' Roll. The movie *White Chicks* (2004) features the Wayans Brothers, two Israelite men in "drag" minstrel roles, and "Niggers with Attitudes" **(NWA was managed by an impostor Jew, Jerry Heller).**

The messages of perverse self-worth, defining success at the price of the soul, normalizing immoral behavior, and corrupt values associated with the images of popular American culture continue to overwhelm the mass media across racial and gender lines. For instances **"Top Model"** may suggest images of beauty as being tall, thin, and blonde. **"I Want a Famous Face"** may send messages that a person's own identity is invalid. In addition, it appears the contemporary trend in liberal Hollywood is the **"Blackout" strategy** where there are no or limited righteous images, stories, shows, heroes, children's television, movies of the descendant of slaves in the mass media. Movies such as ***300, The Ten Commandments, The Passion of Christ, The Maccabees, Noah,*** *and the* ***Exodus*** are the historical stories of the ***Biblical Israelites (ancestors of slaves in the Americas).*** Hollywood's role in belittling and changing narratives of the Israelite holocaust of slavery is expressed in the 1976 movie, *Rocky*. Since the day the Israelites came to the Americas with yokes of iron around their necks, they have been the underdog that had to overcome overwhelming odds of racism in the Americas; however, Rocky is cast as the so-called underdog against the champion Apollo, an Israelite whereas **Apollo** is the real underdog story in the Rocky movies.

    Liberal Hollywood and their American mass media machine continue to blur the blur lines in various social, moral, racial, spiritual, political, and sexual areas to advance their sinister agenda. For instance, the creator and writer of **"Orange is the New Black"**, **Jenji Kohan** (an imposter claiming to be **Jew-*ish***) blurs the blur lines between **equality and morality,** *color and race,* **civil rights and morality**, and *diversity and equality* whereas equality or civil rights is the platform that is used to justify or advocate the immoral behavior of abortion, feminisms, and homosexuality, while trivializing and using the Israelite (Biblical) holocaust of slavery in the Americas as a shield against condemnation. (*i.e. Showtime* **"L" word** *trivializes the horrific effects of slavery's "N" word*). The **Jim Crow Museum of Racist Memorabilia at Ferris State University** trivializes the *holocaust of slavery* when they blur the line between **morality and diversity** by including the plight of all ethnic groups and homosexuals with the plight of our 400-year holocaust of slavery in the Americas. Additionally, Jerry Springer *(****Jew-ish****)* blurred the lines between **justice and injustice** when he aired **"So-called Hate Groups"** with **Hebrew-Israelites vs. KKK** *(i.e. remember the King Kong Kit)* in which the European thugs criminalizes their victims for responding to the horrific crimes of slavery in the Americas. However, I express sympathy with the distress of my people when we continue to witness some of our talented artist like *Prince, Biggie Smalls, Michael Jackson, Tupac, and Whitney Houston, and others' lives* being cut short which reminds me of the values that our Israelite Messiah espoused: **Mark 8:36 "For what shall it profit a man, if he shall gain the whole world, and lose his own soul?"** The historical, social, and spiritual legacy of the American minstrels is that it owned the identity of the descendants of slaves and their story, which was transformed and reduced the Biblical nation of Israel to a BYWORD among the heathens.

Moreover, the impact of the American minstrels continues among the heathens globally. For example, **South Korea** *"The Bubble Sisters & Maikol,"* **Australia** *"Jackson Jive,"* **Netherlands**, *St. Nicholas Day, "Zwarte Piet,"* (Black Pete, based on a Moor from Spain), **Spain** *"Balthazar,"* **Iran** *"Haji Firooz" or "Haj Firuz,"* **Germany**, a **UNICEF 2007** Saving Africa ad featured children in

# BYWORD

burnt cork, **Japan** *"Ganguro," "Gosperats," and "Chibikuro Sambo,"* **Mexico** *"Memin Pinguin,"* **South Africa** *"Coon Carnival",* **Europe** *"Golliwog or Golly,"* **Thailand "Golly",** *Dunkin Donut billboard ad feature faces in burnt cork,* **Brazil** *"Adelaide",* **Columbia** "La Negrita Pulay," "Carnival De Baranquilla," and "Son de Negro," **Peru** *"El Negro Mama,"* and **Venezuela** *"La Negrita."*

There's nothing entertaining about the American White-trash minstrel performers who produced this garbage as a testimony of their immoral values, traditions, envy, and contemptuous enmity for God's chosen people, the Israelites.

The solution for the liberation of the Biblical nation of Israel *(descendant of slaves)* begins with the moral, social, cultural, emotional, and spiritual separation from the heathens and reclaiming their Israelites heritage and values as expressed in their cultural and artistic expression of the Psalms.

**PSALM 137: 1-4**

"By the rivers of Babylon, there we sat down, yea, we wept, when we remembered **Zion**. We hanged our harps upon the willows in the midst thereof. For there they that **carried us away captive** required of us a **SONG**; and they that wasted us required of us mirth, saying, **Sing us**

## Elder Mark Makabi

one of the songs of Zion (i.e. Negro Spirituals). How shall we sing the Lord's song in a strange land?"

## BARBUDANS

**Historical Highlight:** Barbuda became a manufacturing center to grow raw materials, raise stock animals, and breed slaves for Antigua's sugar estates. Moreover, Israelite captives represent more capital than any other assets in the nation including land.

**Origin of the name**: The most popular legend is the name comes from the Portuguese word for "bearded" in conjunction with the fig tree roots resemble beards., similar to the name Barbados.

**Geography**: Caribbean.

**Demographics**: An estimate 94.9% of the population is Israelites (*descendant of slaves including Antigua).*

*Clarifying the blur national, racial, and color lines*: *The so-called Barbudans were transported in slave ships from West Africa to the Americas. Africa is a continent which has fifty-three (53) countries and was most likely named after a Phoenician prefix (Afar) and Latin suffix (ica), speaking the English language, and classifying their national and racial identity after the name of the island which derives from the Portuguese.*

**Barbuda:** Bearded

**Who's Your Father?** Who named Israelite's Barbudans?

**In regards to your national identity, Barbudan is a byword:** Mockery

**Byword guides us back to our nation:**
    Biblical nation of Israel
    Race: Semitic

# BYWORD

Color of skin: Seven shades of brown
Language: Hebrew
Motherland: Jerusalem, Israel

## ANGUILLANS

**Historical Highlight**: Anguilla had a plantation-based economy that produced sugar, rum, cotton, indigo, and mahogany. The genius of the Israelites plantation system was the dominant economic system in the Americas; this is a testimony of the Israelites superior work ethic and horticultural engineering. In the 1700s, the Israelite captives built the "Koal Keel" also known as Warden's place; it was converted into a restaurant in the early 2000s. Emancipation took place on August 1, 1834; the Israelites were freed by 1838.

**Origin of the name**: Spanish word for "eel" which refers to the shape of the island.

**Geography**: Caribbean.

**Demographics**: An estimate 94.7% of the population is Israelites (*descendant of slaves*).

***Clarifying the blur national, racial, and color lines***: *The so-called Anguillans were transported in slave ships from West Africa to the Americas. Africa is a continent which has fifty-three (53) countries and was most likely named after a Phoenician prefix and Latin suffix, speaking the English language, and classifying their national and racial identity after the name of the island that derives from a Spanish word.*

**Anguilla:** Spanish for "eel"**.**

**Who's Your Father?** Who named Israelite's Anguillans?

## Elder Mark Makabi

**In regards to your national identity, Anguillan is a byword:** Ridicule

**Byword guides us back to our nation:**
    Biblical nation of Israel
    Race: Semitic
    Pigmentation: Seven shades of blackness
    Language: Hebrew
    Homeland: Jerusalem, Israel

### AFRO-CHILEANS

**Historical Highlight:** One of the most significant histories for Israelite captives in Chile was their military service. The Israelite captives fought for the Chilean sons of Japheth as members of the 8th regiment of the Andean Liberation Army. The greatest battle took place against the Spanish at Chacabuco, Colombia in 1823. Slavery was abolished in 1823.

**Origin of the name:** There are several theories concerning the origin of the name. One theory is that it derives from Amerindian words such as Quechua "chiri" (cold) and "tchili" meaning "the deepest point of the earth"; the Inca corruption "Tili" (a famous chieftain), or the Mapuche word "chilli" which means "where the land ends."

**Geography:** South America

**Demographics:** An estimate 0.1% of the population is Israelites *(descendant of slaves)*.

***Clarifying the blur national, racial, and color lines:*** The so-called Afro-Chileans were transported in slave ships from West Africa to the Americas. Africa is a continent which has fifty-three (53) countries and was most likely named after a Phoenician prefix

# BYWORD

*(Afar) and Latin suffix (ica), speaking the Spanish language, and classifying their national and racial identity from a word that derived from the natives Indians.*

**Chile**: "Deepest point of the earth."

**Who's Your Father?** Who named Israelite's Afro-Chileans?

**In regards to your national identity, Afro-Chilean is a byword:** Mockery

**Byword guides us back to our nation:**
- Biblical nation of Israel
- Race: Semitic
- Color of skin: Seven shades of brown
- Language: Hebrew
- Motherland: Jerusalem, Israel

## ST. LUCIANS

**Historical Highlight**: St. Lucia was one of the homes of the legendary "Black Caribs."

It was a haven for runaway Israelite slaves who united with the Kalipunas Indians. Together, they aggressively prevented the European Gentile sons of Japheth from colonizing the island until the 18$^{th}$ century. Moreover, the Kalipunas welcomed the Israelites, intermarried with them, and their off springs would become to be known as the **Black Caribs or Garifunas.** By 1777, the Israelites captives represented 84% of the residents. From 1790-1791, the French revolution resulted in freedom for the Israelites captives; however, the British recaptured the island in 1803.

**Origin of the name**: December 13, 1502, French seamen were shipwrecked on the island and named it after the Virgin Martyr of

Syracuse, the so-called saint named "Alousie" or Lucy in honor the pagan feast of Lucy (December 13).

**Geography**: Caribbean.

**Demographics**: An estimate 82.5% of the population is Israelites *(descendant of slaves)*.

***Clarifying the blur national, racial, and color lines***: The so-called St. Lucians were transported in slave ships from West Africa to the Americas. *Africa is a continent which has fifty-three (53) countries and was most likely named after a Phoenician prefix and Latin suffix, speaking the English and French patois languages, and classifying their national and racial identity after the island that was named by the French after a Roman woman.*

**St. Lucia:** named after the so-called virgin martyr, "Alousie" or" Lucy", whom the Europeans presumptuously called a saint. The Children of Israel are the exclusives saints of the most High. Psalm 148:14 (KJV Bible).

**Who's Your Father?** Who named Israelite's St. Lucians?

**In regards to your national identity, St. Lucian is a byword:** Ridicule

**Byword guides us back to our nation:**
    Biblical nation of Israel
    Race: Semitic
    Pigmentation: Seven shades of blackness
    Language: Hebrew
    Homeland: Jerusalem, Israel

## BAHAMIANS

**Historical Highlight**: The Bahamas have a history of pirates, rum runners, boot leggers, slavery, and slave plantations. These European criminals brought their disease of small pox which almost completely extinguished the native population. The Bahamas became a popular island for pirates such as *Edward Teach also known as Black Beard, "Captain"Henry Morgan,* and *Calico Jack Rackham. These are the pirates that America's Hollywood glories while criminalizing the so-called Somali pirates like in the movie Captain Phillips.* Nevertheless, the British brought their Israelite captives to work on sugar plantations. In 1841 a slave revolt resulted in the Israelites taking control of the ship and sailing it to Nassa this event happened two years after Amistad. That same year, slavery was abolished. The disgraceful minstrel comedian, Bert Williams, was born in the Bahamas.

**Origin of the name**: The name derives from the Spanish Baja ("Shallow") mar ("sea") "shallow seas."

**Geography**: Caribbean.

**Demographics**: An estimate of 85% of the population are Israelites *(descendant of slaves).*

***Clarifying the blur national, racial, and color lines****: The so-called Bahamians were transported in slave ships from West Africa to the Americas. Africa is a continent which has fifty-three (53) countries and was most likely named after a Phoenician prefix (Afar) and Latin suffix (ica), speaking the English language, and classifying their national and racial identity after the name of the island that derives from the Spanish for "shallow seas".*

**Bahamia:** "Shallow Sea"

**Who's Your Father?** Who named Israelite's Bahamians?

**In regards to your national identity, Bahamian is a byword:** Mockery

# Elder Mark Makabi

**Byword guides us back to our nation:**
   Biblical nation of Israel
   Race: Semitic
   Color of skin: Seven shades of brown
   Language: Hebrew
   Motherland: Jerusalem, Israel

## AFRO-BOLIVIANS

**Historical Highlight**: There was Israelite slave revolt included an Indian leader *"Juan Santos Atahualpa"* who joined Israelites captives, but was originally a government official assigned to control the Amerindians. The Israelites decided to join with the Amerindian anti-colonial war for freedom. Tupac Amaru (a Mestizo), descendant of the Inca emperors, led the revolt against the Spanish. *Simon Bolivar* fought for the freedom of Israelite captives and **Hipolita** was an enslaved Israelite woman he admired. Slavery was abolished in 1851 and many Israelites settled in Yungas.

**Origin of the name**: The country was named after Simon Bolivar (1783-1830) who was the first President after the country gained its independence in 1825. The Israelites are refer to as Negros, Merones (Brown), Negritos (little black ones), Mullatos (mix-breeds akin to "mule"), and Zambos *(Israelites and Amerindian mixtures.)*

**Geography**: South America.

**Demographics**: An estimate of 1.1% of the population are Israelites *(descendant of slaves)*.

*Clarifying the blur national, racial, and color lines*: *The so-called Afro-Bolivians were transported in slave ships from West Africa to the Americas. Africa is a continent which has fifty-three (53) countries and was most likely named after a Phoenician prefix and Latin suffix, speaking the Spanish language, and classifying their national and racial identity after the name of a man who was considered a Creole (a Spanish man born outside of Spain versus of Israelite mixed descent).*

**Bolivia:** named after Simon Bolivar.

**Who's Your Father?** Who named Israelite's Afro-Bolivians?

**In regards to your national identity, Afro-Bolivian is a byword:** Ridicule

**Byword guides us back to our nation:**

    Biblical nation of Israel

    Race: Semitic

    Pigmentation: Seven shades of blackness

    Language: Hebrew

    Homeland: Jerusalem, Israel

## GRENADIANS

**Historical Highlight**: Julien Fedon was a French plantation owner who became a revolutionary. Although his forces did not take the capital, they were able to crush the opposing force of General Ralph Abercromby. Fedon was able to control Grenada from March 1795 to June 1796. This rebellion is attributed to freedom for all on the island from British tyranny. Slavery was abolished in 1834.

**Origin of the name**: Columbus named this Island "Concepcion" (1498). The origin of the Island name is obscured; however, it is believed that Spanish sailors named the Island after a Spanish state of "Granada", originally a Muslim territory of southern Spain held by Arabs and the Moors (Israelites).

## ELDER MARK MAKABI

**Geography**: Caribbean

**Demographics**: An estimate of 91% of the population are Israelites *(descendant of slaves)*.

*Clarifying the blur national, racial, and color lines: The so-called Grenadians were transported in slave ships from West Africa to the Americas. Africa is a continent which has fifty-three (53) countries and was most likely named after a Phoenician prefix (Afar) and Latin suffix (ica), speaking the English language, and classifying their national and racial identity after the name of the island that was named after a Spanish state.*

**Grenada**: A Spanish city state

**Who's Your Father?** Who named Israelite's Grenadians?

**In regards to your national identity, Grenadian is a byword:** Mockery

**Byword guides us back to our nation:**
    Biblical nation of Israel
    Race: Semitic
    Color of skin: Seven shades of brown
    Language: Hebrew
    Motherland: Jerusalem, Israel

### AFRO-SURINAMESE

**Historical Highlight**: Surinam was the largest northeast colony in South America. In 1667, the Dutch gained control over Surinam from the English where thousands of Israelite slaves worked on sugar and coffee plantations. However, when France occupied Holland from 1795 to 1813, the British took control of Surinam. In 1813, the colony was reinstated to the new Dutch kingdom under Willem I. Thousands of Israelite were imported to Surinam; the *Dutch West Indies Company (DWIC)* priorities depended on the slave trade for their economic development. In 1640, after *Aphra Behn (English woman)* witnessed the brutality of slavery, she became an abolitionist and wrote a book called **"Orronoko"** (Royal slave), published in 1688. It featured an Israelite prince and his Israelite woman "Imoinda" before and after they were sold into slavery. Barend Roelofs petitioned the court for a divorce because his wife Maria Keijser had intimacy with a Negro slave and became pregnant by him.

**Origin of the name**: Named after the Arawaks and Tainos who referred to the land as Surinen.

**Geography**: South America; however, it is considered a Caribbean country.

**Demographics**: An estimate of 39-47% of the population is Israelites *(descendant of slaves also known as Maroons and Creoles)*

***Clarifying the blur national, racial, and color lines***: *The so-called Afro-Surinamese were transported in slave ships from West Africa to the Americas. Africa is a continent which has fifty-three (53) countries and was most likely named after a Phoenician prefix (Afar) and Latin suffix (ica), speaking the Dutch and Sranantongo language, and classifying their national and racial identity after the name given by the Arawak and Taino Amerindians.*

**Suriname:** Name given by the Arawak and Taino.

**Who's Your Father?** Who named Israelite's Afro-Surinamese?

**In regards to your national identity, Afro-Surinam is a byword:** Ridicule

**Byword guides us back to our nation:**

## ELDER MARK MAKABI

Biblical nation of Israel
Race: Semitic
Pigmentation: Seven shades of blackness
Language: Hebrew
Homeland: Jerusalem, Israel

## AFRO-COLOMBIANS

**Historical Highlight**: The "El Son de Negro" carnival is rooted in the same hatred and ignorance of the Israelites found in the American White-trash minstrels. The fraudulent festival displays the figure of an Israelite hero named **Benkos Biohó (Domingo Biohó)**, a *Cimarron*, runaway slave. **Biohó** led an Israelite slaves' resistance movement in Colombia in the early 16th century, ending in a cease fire with the Spanish authorities in 1605 in Cartagena. He established a well-armed, maroon city known as a palenque (a walled city), but was later betrayed and hung in 1619. The city **Biohó** found in the early 1600s became San Basilio de Palenque (also known as the Village of the Maroons or Maroon Village); it was decreed a free city by the Spanish King in 1713. Slavery began to be abolished on May 21, 1851; all Israelites were free by 1857.

A monument of **Benkos Biohó** is erected in Cartagena near the Castillo San Felip de Barajas fortress. In San Basilio de Palenque, there are many streets named after Israelite heroes which is an irregularity in Colombia. Colombia laws requires their schools to commemorate Afro-Colombian National Day on May 21st.

Cartagena was the leading slave market

where Israelite captives were sold. Many Israelites joined with pirates like *Jean Bernard Louis Desjeans and raided alongside Baron de Pointin* in Cartagena in hopes of freedom; however, the French pirates betrayed the slaves and brought them to France.

In modern times, the so-called Afro-Colombians were reported to received so-called reparations for slavery in the form of titles to vast stretches of land; however, because of the vast mineral wealth under their land, President "Alvaro Uribe" violated their human rights and took their land.

**Origin of the name**: This country was named after an Italian *(some believed he was Jewish)* criminal and mass murder named Christopher Columbus; although, he never landed in Columbia. Moreover, the name **Colombeia** most likely refers to the word **"papers" or documents in reference to Columbus**.

**Geography**: South America.

**Demographics**: An estimate of 14-26% of the population is Israelites *(descendant of slaves)*

*Clarifying the blur national, racial, and color lines:* The so-called Afro-Colombians were transported in slave ships from West Africa to the Americas. Africa is a continent which has fifty-three (53) countries and was most likely named after a Phoenician prefix and Latin suffix, speaking the Spanish language, and classifying their national and racial identity after the name of the country that was named after an Italian man.

**Colombia:** Name after Christopher Columbus

**Who's Your Father?** Who named Israelite's Afro-Colombians?

**In regards to your national identity, Afro-Colombian is a byword:** Mockery

# ELDER MARK MAKABI

**Byword guides us back to our nation:**
> Biblical nation of Israel
> Race: Semitic
> Color of skin: Seven shades of brown
> Language: Hebrew
> Motherland: Jerusalem, Israel

**The Willie Lynch Letter (1712)**: *"Our experts warned us about the possibility of this phenomenon occurring, for they say that the mind has a strong drive to correct and re-correct itself over a period of time if it can touch some substantial original historical bases."*

## NEGROES

**Historical Highlight**: What's in a name? A byword can have a demoralizing effect on a group of people lives who collectively respond to it particularly if the name was given to them by their oppressors. In 1712, the making of a "Negro" was documented in the *Willie Lynch letter*. During the slave trade, the European Gentile sons of Japheth reclassified the racial identity of the Israelites via slave codes and their descendants and it became popular to use the term Negro and its derivatives such as nigger. Here lies one of the main bases for the Gentile sons of Japheth to maintain their delusional theory of white supremacy. The social engineering in creating the "Negro myth" continues to be a living testimony for many descendant of slaves that have graduated with honors from the *University of Willie Lynch*.

**Geography**: The United States.

**Demographics**: An estimated of 25 million Israelites in America.

# BYWORD

***Clarifying the blur national, racial, and color lines****: The so-called Negroes were transported in slave ships from West Africa to the Americas. Africa is a continent which has fifty-three (53) countries and was most likely named after a Phoenician prefix (Afar) and Latin suffix (ica), speaking the English language, and classifying their national and racial identity from the Spanish and Portuguese word for the color "black".*

**Negro**: Spanish and Portuguese word for "black"

**Who's Your Father?** Who named Israelite's Negroes?

**In regards to your national identity, Negro is a byword:**

- Ridicule

**Byword guides us back to our nation:**

    Biblical nation of Israel

    Race: Semitic

    Pigmentation: Seven shades of blackness

    Language: Hebrew

    Homeland: Jerusalem, Israel

## BLURRING THE BLUR LINES

*The American White-trash minstrels blurred the lines between color and race, black and white, culture and stereotypes, natural and unnatural, normal and abnormal, love and hate, beautiful and ugly, the truth and the lie,*

*The American White-trash minstrel performers disturbed our groove, diluted our hue, disrupted our mood, distressed our rhythmic groove, corrupted our rules, distorted our cool, distributed our blues, displaced our shoes, but without the rhythm they were asymmetrical fools,*

## Elder Mark Makabi

*The American White-trash minstrels blurred the racial lines, redefined ancient lines, blurred the seeds kind, civil decline, malignant design, corrupted our soul music soul, their Amos and Andy story was brought, and their coon images sold,*

*The American White-trash minstrels performers blurred the color lines, retarded minds, disguised their awe, envied the swing, stole our songs, but could not sing, minstrels didn't mean a thing because they didn't have our Israelite swing,*

*The American White-trash minstrels performers blurred the race lines, polluted the air, hyped their primes, spoiled our rock, regressed our roll, attached our sync, soured our flavor, plunked our pizzazz, distressed our flow, drifted our rhymes, and pimped our crimes, envied our Melanin, revered our hip, and favor our hop,*

***Blackface, burnt-cork minstrels blurred the blur lines between color and colorism, cultural and stereotypical, prejudice and racism, conscience and conscious, success and successful, privileges and freedom;***

*However, Fredrick Douglas articulated his mind, Paul Robeson race was refined, Ella's flow elegantly outshined, the Nicholas Brothers charisma was wisdom designed, Tupac's rhymes: roll the rock from hip to the hop, Cosby's flavor undermined, the wonder of Stevie melodies enshrined the humus reminded, Ali float stung the fear, Denzel acted the typed, Whitney's lifted our voices, Lee spiked the bamboozle, and*

*Michael's walked beat it!*

CHAPTER 7
# THE POWER OF THE NEGRO SPIRITUALS!
"A Biblical Heritage Miraculous Preserved"

**THE FISK JUBILEE ISRAELITE SINGERS 1870**
**The First Family of Music of the Americas!**

Since the day the Arab sons of Ishmael *(Muslims)* sold the children of Israel *(ancestors of the Negro slaves in the Americas)* to the European Christian Gentile sons of Japheth with the assistance of the Edomite sons of Esau *(**Jewish-Israeli**)* who financed the majority of the slave ships that sailed to the Americas, there has been a plot to eradicate the wisdom and identity of the children of slavery Israelite (Biblical) identity in the Americas (specifically the United States). This diabolical plan to erase the name of Israel from the remembrance of their descendants, the slaves in the United States almost succeeded via the *Slave Codes, Black Codes, the religion of slavery, Willie Lynch, American KKK Terrorism, Hollywood movies, NAACP, Civil Rights, American mass media, assimilation, Eugenics, Equality Rights theory, Black Lives Matter, Cesare Borgia, Politics of Inclusions, liberalism, criminality, American music industry, crack cocaine, libertarian, conservatism, Margaret Sanger-Plan Parenthood, Intersectionality, Feminist Movement, the spirit of Sodom & Gomorrah and Byword's;* **however the power of the Negro Spirituals countered this diabolical plan by preserving and documenting the Israelite (Biblical) heritage in a musical format.** What Wisdom! Greatness! Genius! Power! And Glory! Unfortunately, most of the children of the slavery do not recognize, understand, or care about these sacred, secret, priceless, miraculous, and highly spiritual messages that their ancestors continue to communicate to them as a legacy of labor, love, and longevity. **That's sad and disgraceful!**

The Negro Spirituals are rooted in folklore and religion; folklore is the characterization of a nation's traditions, history, culture, religion, celebrations, laws, spirituality, and narratives; these narratives are the oral account in a musical format documenting much of the thoughts and spiritual innovations of the Israelites in the United States. The Negro Spirituals are the narratives of the Israelites. The miracle of the Negro Spirituals is in the understanding that the slaves came from the west coast of Africa, from different tribes, locations, and languages; therefore, how did the Negro Spirituals become the uniform national anthem of all these so-called African tribes in America? *The slaves did not sing about Egypt, the pharaohs, the Ankh, the obelisk, Imhotep Akhenaten, Ramses, Thutmose III, Pyramids, Khufu, King Tut, hieroglyphics, Cleopatra, Ammit, Isis, Ma'at, Horus, Osiris, Aten, Ra, 42 negative confessions, the Central Nile Valley, the capital of Napata and Meroe, Kerma, the book of Coming Forth by Day, or The Book of the Dead, or the Nile River; therefore, they were not Egyptians of Ham also called Kham, related to Khem, Kemitic, nor were they Nubians.*

*The slaves did not sing about Ishmael, Hagar, Mecca, Arabia, the Quran, Mohammad, Allah, or practice Islam; therefore, they were not the sons of Ishamael Arab Muslims. The slaves did not sing about the Kingdom of Axum, the Queen of Sheba, Makeda, Mount Ras Deshen, Abyssinia, Abay River, Cush or Nimrod, the Kebra Nagast; therefore, they were not Ethiopians, Cushites, or Africans. The slaves did not sing about Hanukkah, Bar Mitzvahs, Yom Kippur, Rosh Hashanah, the Khazar Empire, Mount Seir, or the Dukes of Edom; therefore they did not practice Judaism.*

*The slaves did not sing about Ho-Di-No-Sau-Nee, Mud-logs, underground homes, rain dancing, the medicine wheel, sacred-five dancing, the Alognguin language, or a matriarchal society; therefore they were not the natives Anasazi, and/or Native American Indians of the Americas.*

*The slaves did not sing about Christmas Winter New Year, Santa Claus, Easter, Sunday worship, Baptizing backwards, Europe, America, elves, the North Pole, the Roman Cross, Cesare Borgia, praying with their hands clasped together, or popes; therefore, they did not practice Christianity.*

**Kumbayah** is considered the earliest Negro spiritual documented in the United States. The classic Negro Spiritual Kumbayah was translated to *"Com by Yah"* to *"Come by here."* However, when we break-down the language we have **KUM-BA-JAH or KUM-BA-YAH**. *JAH is one of the names that the most High revealed to the Israelites whereas in Hebrew the Y is replace with the J (Psalm 68:4).* Therefore, *"Kum-ba-Jah* or *Kum-ba-yah"* is a song about the Israelites captives crying out to the **God of Abraham, Isaac, and Jacob to be delivered.** The Israelite captives introduced singing and harmony to the world and the American Gentile sons of Japheth, whose musical custom was chanting *(i.e. Gregorian chants)*. Various chanting styles are the musical traditions of nations such as Arabs, Chinese, Iranians, Indians of India, Amerindians or Native American Indians, Europeans, Japanese, Africans, etc. The American Gentile sons of Japheth began to learn how to sing like the Israelite captives by picking up on their musical vibrations, *"feeling their vibes"*, and then reclassified their Negro spirituals as Christian music. The historical and corrupted traditions of the American sons of Japheth stealing the heritage of the Israelites captives and placing a white face on it is well documented throughout European, American, and Israelite histories. For example *Thomas "Daddy" Rice became rich and famous by* imitating *the vibes of an Israelite slave singing a song called* **"Jump Jim Crow"**. *Stephen Foster became successful from the vibes of the slaves songs to write white-trash minstrel tunes. Fred Astaire picked the vibrations of the great Israelite dancer,* **Bill "Bo Jangles" Robinson**. *Elvis Presley learned from*

# BYWORD

the vibrations *"**Arthur "Big Boy" Crudup**", the true Israelite father of Rock and Roll. Tom Jones imitated the vibes from one of the Israelite fathers of soul "**Solomon Burke,**" "**Brook Brenton,**" and "**Jackie Wilson.**"*

*Jerry Lee Lewis imitated the vibes from* **"Little Richard"**. *Dean Martin imitated the vibes of* **"Harry Mills" of the Mills Brothers.** *The Osmond Brothers imitated the vibes of the "***Jackson 5".** *The Beatles learned to vibe from one of the Israelite fathers of Rock and Roll* **"Little Richard" and "Chuck Berry."** *In addition, The Rolling Stones imitated the vibes of* **McKinley "Muddy Waters Morganfield , "Chester "Howling Wolf", Arthur Burnett and Bo Diddley"** *Eric Clapton imitated learned to vibe from his masters* **John Lee Hooker** *and* **the Grandfather of Rock** *and* **Roll "Robert Johnson".** *Eddie Van Halen and a whole host of Caucasian guitarists admired the vibes of* **"Jimi Hendrix."** *Eminem and Iggy Azalea are trying to imitate the Hip-hop vibes from Kendrick Lamar, Ben Blackwell, Israelite Boy, Run DMC, Nas, KRS-One, Peeze & Shod, The Deacon, and Sister Souljah. Hank Williams, Sr. and Jr. learned to vibes from his master teacher and the true* **Father of Country music, "Rufus Tee-Tot Payne**,*" Honoring the "Mothers of Rock and Roll "Rosetta Tharpe," and Willie Mae "Big Mama" Thornton. Melania Trump allegedly plagiarized Michelle Obama's speech at the GOP Convention Cleveland, OH July 18, 2016.*

The Negro spirituals are Israelites' folklore that demonstrates the rhythms, songs, dances, and cultural expressions of our ancient He-

# ELDER MARK MAKABI

brew-Israelites fathers. For example Chuck Berry "Maybelline" is equivalent to listening to the rock song of Moses (Exodus 15). King David danced like Michael Jackson, the soulful voice of Althea Franklin parallels Miriam's soulful voice, the vibes of Tupac vibes with King Solomon Songs, the Jazz trumpet of Louis Armstrong express the Levites blowing the trumpet's in the new moon, and the Gospel's sounds of Mahalia Jackson is in accord with the Daughters of Zion gospel-sounding orations. **The fact that the slaves were singing the Negro spirituals for nearly two-hundred (200) years on the plantations before the masses of American sons of Japheth heard them proves that these miraculous spirituals were not contaminated or influenced by the American Sons of Japheth Christianity which is why they are called "The Negro Spirituals."**

In 1870, George White played a central role as the manager of the Fisk Jubilee Israelite Singers along with assisting in the preservation of the Negro Spirituals. Such endeavors made it possible for the Jubilee Israelite Singers to tour America and abroad. The Fisk Jubilee-Israelite singers dazzled audience all over the world with their electrifying performance to raise money to build a school for the emancipated Israelite slaves and they used their God-given talent to restore dignity and respect to Israelite people in the Americas. The Fisk Jubilee-Israelite singers are models for us to emulate. We must emulate these singers by actively using our God-given musical talents. Moreover, the descendants of slaves should understand the power of music with which God blesses them. This talent is not to be used to corrupt, be driven by money, fame, power, greed, or to sell souls for vanity and the degradation of their people. Musical talents are to be performed **"to praises the most High and honor thy father and thy mother [ancestors] that your days may be prolonged on the earth"** (Exodus 20:12).

### "A Biblical Heritage Miraculous Preserved"

- "Go Down Moses" Let My People Go!
- "Joshua fit the battle of Jericho"
- "When the Saints Go Marching In"
- "Steal Away"
- "Rivers of Babylon"
- "Blow your Trumpet Gabriel"
- "Ezekiel saw the Wheel"
- "Didn't my Lord Deliver Daniel?"
- "Swing Low"
- "Wade in the Water!"
- "Precious Lord, Take My Hand!"
- "Twelve Gates to the City!"
- "Bound for Canaan Land"
- "Daniel saw the Stone"
- "Dry Bones"
- "Get away Jordan"
- "Ride on Moses"

The success of the *Fisk Jubilee-Israelite Singers* and the Negro Spirituals prompted the American billion dollar music industry and the Jubilee-Israelite singers became the model of success for the

American recording industry. Moreover, the genius of the Israelite musician and his music became a phenomenon *in the United States, all of North and South America, the Caribbean, and worldwide. Ragtime, Jazz, Blues, Country, Soul, Rhythm and Blues, Gospel, Bebop, Boogie Woogie, Swing, Caribbean Music, Calypso, Rumba, Salsa, Neo-Soul, Pop, Dance, Club, Funk, Reggae, Disco, Rock & Roll, and Hip-Hop all arose from the Israelites in the Americas and their "Negro spirituals".*

Hip-hop is synonymous with the Negro spirituals because it is the modern-day social awareness platform for the Israelites (**e.g. Let My People Go becomes Public Enemy's Fight the Power)** In addition, the Negro Spirituals were secret codes and created by the Israelite captives in a number of dialects to communicate plots against their enemies and many other social, moral, and spiritual issues pertaining to their captivity in the land of the so-called free. For example **"*Steal Away Jesus*"** is a song about the Israelite captives stealing the ship named "Jesus" to escape and sail away; therefore, when the slaves sung about Jesus, it was primarily metaphoric. The metaphor of the ship sailing referred to a vessel of freedom and salvation, a return back to the Israelite homeland and the advancements and glory of Israelite culture *The principal message of power that the Negro Spirituals exemplify is the knowledge of self, affirms the Negro myth, and the refutation of the lies spread by the Edomites and European sons of Japheth, specifically that the slaves were savages in jungles who needed to be so-called civilized and Christianized (i.e. Hellenized) under the Anti-Semitic American institution of racism and slavery.*

The United States of America models its legal court structure, primarily the supreme and state courts, the legal insights and instructions established by the Israelite prophet Moses. *Furthermore,* ***The Magna Carter (1215), The Petition of Rights (1628), The U.S. Constitution (1787)****, the French Declaration of the Rights of Man and the Citizen (1789), and the American "Bill of Rights" (1791), and the United Nations "Universal Declaration of Human Rights" (1948)* *are replicas of the* "**Cyrus Cylinder**" (539 B.C.) *from the Persian King Cyrus*. **However, it was the Israelite Daniel that orchestrated, influence, and inspired the Cyrus Cylinder because he guided, influenced, and instructed King Cyrus with the knowledge, understanding, and wisdom of the moral code of human righteousness and dignity that led King Cyrus to let the Israelite captives to leave Babylon as a free nation.** It is reported that the first charter on human rights, the "Cyrus Cylinder", is on the second floor of the United Nations and written in Hebrew. The American jury system of twelve (12) jurors is model after the 12 Judges of the 12 tribes of Israel moreover, the Israelites understood the medical principles of cleanliness which is the foundation of medical science. American modern medical books acknowledge one of the fathers of medicine, Moses (**Surgical Technology for the Surgical Technologist: A Positive Care Approach 2nd edition**) Furthermore, the **Israelites contribute to the development of the alphabet under the leadership of Moses (i.e. commencing with the 10 Commandments)** which was transported by the Phoenicians (a Black-Hamitic people) to the Greeks; therefore, the modern day writing system is based on another great contribution by the Israelites. Many Israelites (i.e. Daniel, Isaiah etc.) had advanced scientific knowledge and understanding that the earth was flat with a circular circumference. **Furthermore, the United States of America and many other European nations stole the national colors from the Israelites: RED, WHITE, BLUE, AND PURPLE (the Romans stole the color purple in 70 AD).**

The Israelites introduced their spectacular culinary skills as **soul food,** *which include Jamaican food; however excluding unclean foods. (i.e. Pork - Leviticus 11).* This later was popularized by Southern-style cuisine. Allegations still surround the fact that Colonel Sanders developed his Kentucky Fried Chicken brand based on watching and observing Israelite people eating in their cars along the road due to Jim Crow. Once, the so-called Colonel got hold of the basic recipe for pressure cooking and frying, he introduced so-called White America to Israelite cuisine but with a less potent taste of culinary experience. Our unique flavor, recipes, and seasoning of our *soul food cuisine* was documented since 1446 B.C. (*Leviticus 2:13 "And every oblation of thy* **meat offering shalt thou season with salt;"***).*

The American music industry, the recording artist, industry professionals, music fans, the American people, and the world owe homage and tribute to the *Fisk Jubilee-Israelite singers, Israelites, and George White for* introducing the *Biblical folklores of the Negro Spirituals to the world.* Therefore, the **Fisk Jubilee-Israelite Singers "Awards"** (*not the Grammys*) should be the standard for musical and moral achievements. This atonement would be in honor of the contributions of *"the first family of music in the Americas"* **which preserved the Israelite (Biblical) heritage within the Negro spirituals**... the basis for the billion-dollar American music industry. The confederate of the Ishmaelite's, (Arabs) Edomite's, (Jewish)

## BYWORD

and the Christians Gentiles (Caucasians) mischievous plan to erase the Israelite identity from the descendants of the Negro slaves was countered by the power of the Negro spirituals which preserve their Israelite national identity in a lyrical and musical format (Psalm 84:1-4).

### THE UNITED STATES OF AMERICA HOUSE OF REPRESENTATIVE DECLARES:
### "THE NEGRO SPIRITUALS NATIONAL TREASURES"

"On February 7, 2007, The House of Representatives passed Bill # H Res. 120 recognizing the Negro Spirituals as a National Treasure

### BONAIRIANS

**Historical Highlight**: The native "Caiquetios" were the original inhabits of the land before *Alonso de Ojeda and Amerigo Vespucci* arrived in 1499. Bonaire was settled in 1526 and became a center for raising animals most likely by European convicts from other Spanish colonies. In addition, Bonaire became a plantation island for the Dutch West Indies Company.

**Origin of the name**: The origin of the name is uncertain; however, it is believed the name derives from the Caiquetio word "bonay" meaning "low country". The Spanish and Dutch modified its spelling to Bojna and Bonaire.

**Geography**: Caribbean, the ABC Islands (Aruba, Bonaire, and Curacao)

**Demographics**: An estimate of 85% of the population are Israelites *(descendant of slaves which includes intermarriages within the six islands).*

***Clarifying the blur national, racial, and color lines****: The so-called Bonairians were transported in slave ships from West Africa to the Americas. Africa is a continent which has fifty-three (53) countries and was most likely named after a Phoenician prefix and Latin suffix, speaking the Dutch, English, and Papiarmentu language, and classifying their national and racial identity after the name of the island that is most likely named after an Amerindian tribe.*

**Bonaire:** "Low land"

**Who's Your Father?** Who named Israelite's Bonairians?

**In regards to your national identity, Bonairian is a byword:** Ridicule

**Byword guides us back to our nation:**
    Biblical nation of Israel
    Race: Semitic
    Pigmentation: Seven shades of blackness
    Language: Hebrew
    Homeland: Jerusalem, Israel

## WEST INDIANS

**Historical Highlight**: The region comprises more than 7,000 islands, islets, reefs, and cays in which these islands are called the West Indies after being discovered as not part of the East Indies in Southeast Asia.

**Origin of the name**: the original inhabitants were the Kalipuna and Arawak Indians. Christopher Columbus gave the West Indies its name because he believed he reached islands near India.

# BYWORD

**Geography**: Caribbean (over 7,000 islands)

**Demographics**: Israelites remnant scattered *(descendant of slaves)*

*Clarifying the blur national, racial, and color lines*: The so-called West Indians were transported in slave ships from West Africa to the Americas. Africa is a continent which has fifty-three (53) countries and was most likely named after a Phoenician prefix (Afar) and Latin suffix (ica), speaking various European languages, and classifying their national and racial identity from invalid geographical location named by an Italian who believed he was in India.

**West Indies:** An archipelago between southeast North America and northern South America.

**Who's Your Father?** Who named Israelite's West Indians?

**In regards to your national identity, West Indian is a byword:** Mockery

**Byword guides us back to our nation:**
    Biblical nation of Israel
    Race: Semitic
    Color of skin: Seven shades of brown
    Language: Hebrew
    Motherland: Jerusalem, Israel

The second president in Egypt Gamal Abdel Nasser (1956) appeared on radio and television, addressing the Edomite Jewish sons of Esau and the European sons of Japheth, *"You have left Black and returned White you are impostors and shall never see peace," from* The End of the Jewish People by Georges Friedmann.

## HISPANICS

**Historical Highlight**: Hispanic has various definitions. There seems to be no absolute consensus on the meaning of Hispanic; however, the general agreement of the term is that Hispanic refers to the Spanish, their history and culture and/or an American whose first language is Spanish. This term can be misleading; for example, a descendant of slaves that speaks Spanish *(e.g. Afro-Cubans, Afro-Colombians, etc.)* can be racial classified as Hispanic because he or she speaks Spanish which would be contrary to their Israelite heritage.

**Origin of the name**: Hispanic derives from the Latin *Hispanicus*, and *Hispania* (the Iberian Peninsula).

**Geography**: Caribbean, Hispaniola

**Demographics**: An estimate of 17% U.S. population are so-called Hispanics according to the U.S. Census Bureau (July 2015).

***Clarifying the blur national, racial, and color lines***: *The so-called Afro-Hispanics were transported in slave ships from West Africa to the Americas. Africa is a continent which has fifty-three (53) countries and was most likely named after a Phoenician prefix and Latin suffix, speaking the Spanish language, and classifying their national and racial identity after an adopted European classification for Spanish heritage.*

**Hispanic:** Pertaining to Spain.

**Afro-Hispanic/Hispanics**: Individuals who identify themselves as Hispanics of European and/or European mix with Amerindians descent are not Israelites.

**One Drop Rules! Negro Blood:** Historically, it was custom for most mixed race people of Israelite, Amerindian, and European descent to deny their so-called Negro blood in order to improve their social and economic status in the Americas. Moreover, the European sons of Japheth understood that one drop of the Negro blood was superior because the so-called Negro gene (a blessing to the Israelites from God) was and remains dominant over the genes of the recessive genes of the Gentile Europeans. Therefore the Gentiles European sons of Japheth classified a person with one drop of Israelite (Biblical) blood as a "Negro", Spanish for the color "black" and a misnomer of the Israelite people in the Americas. Nevertheless, in the near future it will be very popular or expedient for many nations to apply the one drop rule as a direct link to the Biblical Israelites.

**Who's Your Father?** Who named Israelite's Afro-Hispanics?

**In regards to your national identity, Afro-Hispanic is a byword:** Ridicule

**Byword guides us back to our nation:**
- Biblical nation of Israel
- Race: Semitic
- Pigmentation: Seven shades of blackness
- Language: Hebrew
- Homeland: Jerusalem, Israel

## BRITISH VIRGIN ISLANDERS

**Historical Highlight**: Slavery was a major part of the British Virgin Islands. Furthermore, the British won control of the island between the Danes and the Dutch. Treatment of the Israelites was extremely harsh with regular whippings, beatings, and killings; this caused many revolts at the Isaac Pickering, George Nibb, and Lettsome plantations.

**Origin of the name**: Christopher Columbus named this Island after Ursula and her 11,000 martyred virgins who died at the hands of Attila the Hun.

**Geography**: Caribbean, consisting of four larger islands, Tortola, Anegada, Virgin Gorda, and Jost Van Dyke, and 32 smaller islands and inlets of which 20 are uninhabited.

**Demographics**: An estimate of 83% of the population are Israelites *(descendant of slaves).*

*Clarifying the blur national, racial, and color lines: The so-called Virgin Islanders were transported in slave ships from West Africa to the Americas. Africa is a continent which has fifty-three (53) countries and was most likely named after a Phoenician prefix (Afar) and Latin suffix (ica), speaking the English language, and classifying their national and racial identity after a name of the island that an Italian named after a British princess.*

**British Virgin Islanders:** Named after **European** woman Ursula and her 11,000 martyred virgins.

**British Virgin Islands:** 36 islands; 16 are inhabited.

**Who's Your Father?** Who named Israelite's Virgin Islanders?

**In regards to your national identity, Virgin Islander is a byword:** Mockery

**Byword guides us back to our nation:**
    Biblical nation of Israel
    Race: Semitic
    Color of skin: Seven shades of brown
    Language: Hebrew
    Motherland: Jerusalem, Israel

## NIGGER

**Origins of the name:** The super byword **(insult)** has had a demoralizing effect on the children of slavery and the American sons of Japheth. "niger" in the Latin language simply means "black", and

## BYWORD

in Spanish it became the noun Negro *(black person)*. The Israelite prophets and the disciples of *Jesus the Christ* his kinsman were called **NIGERS** *(including Luke and Paul, the Apostle also known as Saul)* in **Acts 13:1.** The carnal minds of the *sons of Japheth (Caucasians)* phonetically and morally corrupted *"niger"* which led to its mispronunciation as nigger which has become morally synonymous with dehumanization, nonpersons, self-hate, and a primary symbol of America's racism.

- **Niger Geography**: Niger and Nigeria are in West Africa's Sahara region where many Israelites sojourned and associated with commerce; that is why they were identified as NIGER BLACK in ACTS 13:1
- **Niger River:** The third longest river in Africa after the Nile and Congo.

**Demographics**: Estimated 200 million Israelites in the Americas.

*Clarifying the blur national, racial, and color lines:* The so-called Niggers were transported in slave ships from West Africa to the Americas. Africa is a continent which has fifty-three (53) countries and was most likely named after a Phoenician prefix and Latin suffix, speaking various European languages, and classifying their national and racial identity after a Latin word that means "black" and expressing the phonetical ineptness of American sons of Japheth enunciation aptitude of the word "niger".

**Acts 13:1:** "Now there were in the church that was at Antioch certain **prophets and teachers**; as **Barnabas, and Simeon** [Israelites] that was called **NIGER** and Lucius of Cyrene (Luke), and

Manaen, which had been brought up with Herod the tetrarch, and **Saul."** *(Saul is Paul the Apostle Romans 11:1)*

- **Negus:** king, ruler, or emperor in the Ethiopian language (Amharic)
- **Niger:** derives from the Latin language meaning black.

**Who's Your Father?** Who named Israelite's Niggers?

**The corruption of Niger to Nigger has evolved into a super byword: Insult**

**Byword guides us back to our nation:**
- Biblical nation of Israel
- Race: Semitic
- Pigmentation: Seven shades of blackness
- Language: Hebrew
- Homeland: Jerusalem, Israel

## AFRO-ARGENTINES

**Historical Highlight**: In 1580, Argentina was a center for contraband trade in which silver was exchanged for Israelite slaves. In 1813 slavery was abolished and many Israelites served in the Liberator Amy in 1817. However, in recent history, Argentina has been known to be a country that is terribly Anti-Semitic concerning the descendants of the Hebrews slaves within that country and abroad.

**Origin of the name**: The name derives from the Latin word "argentum" meaning "silver".

**Geography**: South America.

**Demographics**: An estimate of 5 % of the population are Israelites *(descendant of slaves)*.

***Clarifying the blur national, racial, and color lines***: *The so-called Afro-Argentines were transported in slave ships from West Africa to the Americas. Africa is a continent which has fifty-three (53) countries and was most likely named after a Phoenician prefix (Afar) and Latin suffix (ica), speaking the Spanish language, and classifying their national and racial identity after the name of the land that the Spanish named from the Latin language.*

**Afro**: An abbreviation for African or referring to a hairstyle in the 1960s and 1970s in the United States. The afro reflected pride, glory, and proactive self-awareness among the Israelite descendants of slaves in the Americas.

**Argentina:** "Silver".

**Anti-Semitic Racism:** worldwide institutions that systematically dehumanized and violate the human rights of the Israelites *(the descendant of slaves)* in every aspect of its society.

**Who's Your Father?** Who named Israelite's Afro-Argentines?

**In regards to your national identity, Afro-Argentine is a byword:** Mockery

**Byword guides us back to our nation:**
    Biblical nation of Israel
    Race: Semitic
    Color of skin: Seven shades of brown
    Language: Hebrew
    Motherland: Jerusalem, Israel

# Elder Mark Makabi

## AFROMESTIZO-SALVADORANS

**Historical Highlight:** In 1526, Pedro de Alvarado founded the capital city of San Salvador. In 1541, Israelite captives where imported from Africa into El Salvador; even though, the *"New Laws"* ended forced labor of the native Amerindians. An estimate of 10,000 Israelites were brought to work on the haciendas and in the mines of El Salvador (1548). Indigo *(blue dye)* became a fundamental export which established economic development of towns based on slave plantations such as *Sonsonate, Santa Ana Zacatecolus, Chinameca, Ahuachapan, San Miguel, and San Salvador.* The mixing of *Israelite slaves, Amerindians, and the Spanish created free "mulattos" and "Zambos."* The Israelite dances *"Cumbia,"* the *Rumbia-Bolero,* and the *"merengue"* developed in El Salvador.

**Origins of the name:** During their conquest the Spanish conquistadors, the land was named "El Salvador", which means "Savior" named after Jesus.

**Geography**: Central America.

**Demographics**: An estimated of 90% of the population are mestizos, which means "mixed" *(Natives Indians and Spaniards)*. However, historically, most Mestizo have denied their Israelite blood. The Zambos are a mixture of Israelite slaves and natives Indians whereas the mulattos are mixture of Israelite slaves, Spaniards, and natives. *The Pipil or Pokoman, Maya, and Lenca were the natives.*

*Clarifying the blur national, racial, and color lines*: *The so-called Afro-Salvadorans were transported in slave ships from West Africa to the Americas. Africa is a continent which has fifty-three (53) countries and was most likely named after a Phoenician prefix and Latin suffix, speaking the Spanish language, and classifying their national and racial identity after the name of land that was named by the Spanish for "the savior."*

**Salvadorans**: Named for "Savior".

**Zambos**: Children of intermarriage between Israelite slaves and Amerindian natives.

**Who's Your Father?** Who named Israelite's Afromestizo Salvadorans or Zamos?

**In regards to your national identity, Afromestizos is a byword:** Ridicule

**Byword guides us back to our nation:**

Biblical nation of Israel

Race: Semitic

Pigmentation: Seven shades of blackness

Language: Hebrew

Homeland: Jerusalem, Israel

## GUATEMALANS-GARIFUNA

**Historical Highlight:** the Garifunas were exiled to the island Roatan in 1787 by the British. James Derhame was born into slavery (1762), but became a doctor and inventor. Slavery was abolished in 1823.

**Origins of the name:** the name derives from the Mayan Indians meaning "place of forests or many trees."

**Geography**: Central America.

**Locations of the Garifuna:** Caribbean, Belize, Guatemala, St. Vincent, Nicaragua, Honduras, and Roatan.

**Demographics**: An estimated of 1.0 % or 200,000 of the populations are Israelites *(the descendant of slaves).*

## ELDER MARK MAKABI

***Clarifying the blur national, racial, and color lines****:* The so-called Guatemalans Garifuna were transported in slave ships from West Africa to the Americas. Africa is a continent which has fifty-three (53) countries and was most likely named after a Phoenician prefix (Afar) and Latin suffix (ica), speaking the Spanish and English languages, and classifying their national and racial identity after the name of the land that derives from the Mayan Indian word for "place of forests or many trees".

**Guatemala**: Place of forest or many trees.

**Garifuna:** Children of intermarriage between the Israelites and Amerindians became the Garifuna or Karaphuna. There is a debate about the definition Gari which is believed to translate to food or "cassava-eating people".

**Who's Your Father?** Who named Israelite's Guatemalans or Garifuna?

**In regards to your national identity, Guatemalans-Garifuna is a byword:** Mockery

**Byword guides us back to our nation:**
- Biblical nation of Israel
- Race: Semitic
- Color of skin: Seven shades of brown
- Language: Hebrew
- Motherland: Jerusalem, Israel

### SABAN

**Histrocal Highlight:** Curacao (Korsow), Bonaire, Sint Eustatius, Saba, and Sint Maarten are the Netherland Antilles where Israelite captives worked on the slave plantations. Curacao and

# BYWORD

Sint Eustatius became centers for European thugs such as pirates, smugglers, rapist, murders, theives, and slave traders. Curacao and Bonaire never developed plantations because of the arid climate. Slavery was abloshed in 1863.

**Origins of the name:** the name derives from the Arawak tribes who called the island "Siba" meaning "rock" or Sheba meaning "morning".

**Geography**: Caribbean.

**Demographics**: An estimate of 85% of the population is Israelites (descendant of slaves) on the six islands of Bonaire, Curacao, Saba, Sint Eustatius, Sint Maarten, and Aruba.

*Clarifying the blur national, racial, and color lines: The so-called Sabans were transported in slave ships from West Africa to the Americas. Africa is a continent which has fifty-three (53) countries and was most likely named after a Phoenician prefix and Latin suffix, speaking the Dutch language, and classifying their national and racial identity after the name of the land that derived from the Arawaks.*

**Saba:** "The Rock"

**Who's Your Father?** Who named Israelite's Sabans?

**In regards to your national identity, Saban is a byword:** Ridicule

**Byword guides us back to our nation:**
    Biblical nation of Israel
    Race: Semitic
    Pigmentation: Seven shades of blackness
    Language: Hebrew
    Homeland: Jerusalem, Israel

# Elder Mark Makabi

## AFRO- ECUADORIANS

**Historical Highlight:** The Inca Empire was established before the Europeans Gentile sons of Japheth arrived; however, the Europeans brought epidemics of diseases such as the measles, influenza, and smallpox to Ecuador which killed many of the natives.

*Esmeraida also known as the "Black Province"* is where most Israelites reside. Israelite captives reached Quito, Ecuador in 1533. Many escaped from stranded ships and established maroon settlements which became safe havens for escaped Israelite slaves. There is the story of twelve Israelites off Cape Francisco that escaped from a stranded slave ship, killed the surviving Spanish, and established their kingdom among the natives. For example, Alonso de Illescas was an Israelite chief of such a settlement. Jose Maria Urbina freed the slaves and recruited many of them in the military; the Israelite *Azarye* became a senior general in 1851.

**Origins of the name:** Ecuador is Spanish for "equator".

**Geography:** South America

**Demographics:** An estimated of 3- 8% the populations is Israelites *(the descendants of slaves)*

*Clarifying the blur national, racial, and color lines*: The so-called Afro-Ecuadorians were transported in slave ships from West Africa to the Americas. Africa is a continent which has fifty-three (53) countries and was most likely named after a Phoenician prefix (Afar) and Latin suffix (ica), speaking the Spanish language, and classifying their national and racial identity after a land that was named by the Spanish.

**Ecuador:** Spanish for "Equator"

**Who's Your Father?** Who named Israelite's Afro-Ecuadorians?

# BYWORD

**In regards to your national identity, Afro-Ecuadorian is a byword:** Mockery

**Byword guides us back to our nation:**

    Biblical nation of Israel

    Race: Semitic

    Color of skin: Seven shades of brown

    Language: Hebrew

    Motherland: Jerusalem, Israel

### Elder Mark Makabi

# SAINT ERNESTINE
#### Mark-Alan

*The mountain of my mother is exalted on this day
and living waters flow from
the fountains of her heart,
By the rivers of her green pastures,
through her house into her home,
Express by the fruits from her vine,
The wings of my mother will soar on this day,
And the graceful power of the rushing winds
will ride under her wings,
From the hearts of many who loved her,
across the seas,
above the hills, and to the sky's limit,
where stars congregate, nightfall rests,
And the floras moonbeam penetrates
emotions' progenitor's cycles,*

### *SAINT ERNESTINE, MY BIRTHDAY BLESSING!*
#### September 19, 1930

# BYWORD

## TURKS & CAICOS ISLANDERS "BELONGERS"

**Historical Highlight:** A British colony with 40 islands; 8 are inhabited. Pirates lived on the island as bases to attack Spanish ships. Turks and Caicos were the salt industry producers of the Caribbean economy. From 1767 to 1781, the royal regulations stated that Israelite captives were not permitted to work on their own salt ponds. The Israelites exodus from the island began during the Haitian Revolution in 1791. TCI continues to ponder their national identity.

**Origins of the name:** The popular theory is Turk derives from the native Turk's Head or "fez" cactuses; Caicos is a Lucayan term, "caya hico," which means "string of Islands." Another theory is that the pirate history of the "Island Turk" translates to "Pirate Island" referring to the Ottoman Turks who terrorized much of Mediterranean Europe and North Africa!

**Geography**: Caribbean; British West Indies, 40 islands

**Demographics**: An estimated of 90% the populations are Israelites *(the descendants of slaves)*.

*Clarifying the blur national, racial, and color lines: The so-called Belongers were transported in slave ships from West Africa to the Americas. Africa is a continent which has fifty-three (53) countries and was most likely named after a Phoenician prefix and Latin suffix, speaking the English language, and classifying their national and racial identity after the name of the island which derives from the natives or the Europeans who named one of the islands after so-called pirates.*

**Turks**: Turk Head fez cactus or pirate.

**Caicos:** String of islands.

## ELDER MARK MAKABI

**Who's Your Father?** Who named Israelite's "Belongers" of the Turks & Caicos Islands?

**In regards to your national identity, "Belongers" is a byword:** - Mockery

**Byword guides us back to our nation:**
  Biblical nation of Israel
  Race: Semitic
  Pigmentation: Seven shades of blackness
  Language: Hebrew
  Homeland: Jerusalem, Israel

## HAITIANS

**Historical Highlight**: The Israelite general, ***Saint Toussaint L'Ouveture (1743-1803)*** defeated Napoleon. Saint Toussaint was an Israelite captive, self-educated, and with no military training; however, he overthrew the French and led his people to freedom. ***Saint Toussaint L'Ouveture the Great*** annihilated the French chattel slavery system between *1791 and 1794*; many European slave owners, women, and children were put to death. Haiti was the first country in the Americas to abolish slavery. Jean Jacques Dessalines (1758-1806) was known as a former Israelite captive who served under Toussaint L'Ouverture. Dessalines became Governor of Haiti and had the Declaration of Independence written in 1804. He then crowned himself Emperor; however, he was killed by assassination in October 1806.

**Origin of the name**: The original named *"Ayiti"* was given by the Arawak and Taino; however the so-called Haitians modified the spelling to Haiti as a symbol of their independence from France (1804). Haiti (Ayiti) means "mountainous or big land".

# BYWORD

**Geography**: Caribbean.

**Demographics**: An estimate 90% of the population are Israelites *(the descendant of slaves)*.

***Clarifying the blur national, racial, and color lines****: The so-called Haitians were transported in slave ships from West Africa to the Americas. Africa is a continent which has fifty-three (53) countries and was most likely named after a Phoenician prefix (Afar) and Latin suffix (ica), speaking the French Creole language, and classifying their national and racial identity after the name of the island that derives from the Arawaks/Tanios natives.*

**Haiti:** "mountainous land and/or mountains" or "bird land".

**Who's Your Father?** Who named Israelite's Haitians?

**In regards to your national identity, Haitian is a byword:** Ridicule

**Byword guides us back to our nation:**

    Biblical nation of Israel

    Race: Semitic

    Color of skin: Seven shades of brown

    Language: Hebrew

    Motherland: Jerusalem, Israel

## BLACK SEMINOLES

**Historical Highlight:** The Israelites that escaped to freedom in Florida were great warriors. These self-emancipated Israelites intermarried with the Seminoles Indians; their children were called the *"Black Seminoles". The Seminoles and the Black Seminoles* fought together against *Andrew Jackson in 1818,* but were defeated and driven into remote southern regions of Florida. However,

## Elder Mark Makabi

the Black Seminoles lead a fierce resistance against General Jesup for six years using guerilla warfare tactics during the Second War with the U.S. Army. Furthermore, the U.S. Army captured Black Seminoles leaders and removed them, sending them to the west. Later, after the Civil War, the U.S. cavalry in southern Texas recruited Black Seminoles in the army as scouts; three of the Black Seminoles scouts won the Congressional Medal of Honor. *One of the greatest Black Seminoles was* **"John Horse"** *a great Israelite (1812-1882).*

**Origins of the name:** The Americans called Florida Indians "Seminoles" which derived from the Spanish word "Cimarron". Cimarron means "an untamed fugitive"; *Israelites and Seminoles intermarried* and bore the ***"Black Seminoles."***

**Geography**: North America, southern Florida

**Demographics**: Israelites remnant scattered in America.

***Clarifying the blur national, racial, and color lines:*** The Black Seminoles were transported in slave ships from West Africa to the Americas. Africa is a continent which has fifty-three (53) countries and was most likely named after a Phoenician prefix and Latin suffix, speaking the English and Creole languages, and classifying their national and racial identity as a color and from a word that derives from Spanish.

**Black or Brown:** Pigmentation relating to skin.

**Seminoles:** from the Spanish word "Cimarron", meaning untamed fugitive.

**Native American Indians and Hispanics:** to proclaim that the Natives Americans Indians and Hispanics are Israelites without qualifying them is an error.

# BYWORD

**Who's Your Father?** Who named Israelite's "Black Seminoles"?

**In regards to your national identity, Black Seminole is a Byword:** Mockery

**Byword guides us back to our nation:**
- Biblical nation of Israel
- Race: Semitic
- Pigmentation: Seven shades of blackness
- Language: Hebrew
- Homeland: Jerusalem, Israel

## ANTIGUANS

**Historical Highlight:** Antigua was one of the most profitable colonies for the British in the Caribbean. In 1672, 570 Israelites captives were transported to the island, and by 1674 Israelites captives represented half of the population. Although Israelites were captives, they were impudent causing the slave owners fears of revolution. In 1729, a plot to kill all European Gentile sons of Japheth was discovered and two Israelites were burned alive. In 1736, slaves were charged with conspiracy were tormented, tortured, broken on the wheel, gibbeted alive on gallows and stakes. Slavery was abolished on August 1, 1834, now celebrated at the *Carnival of Antigua*.

**Origin of the name**: Columbus named the island "Santa Maria de la Antigua" in honor the Biblical "Saint Virgin Mary of the Ancient Times", originally an Israelite woman of color (1493).

**Geography**: Caribbean.

**Demographics**: An estimate of 94.9% of the population are Israelites *(the descendant of slaves which includes Barbuda)*.

## ELDER MARK MAKABI

***Clarifying the blur national, racial, and color lines****:* The so-called Antiguans were transported in slave ships from West Africa to the Americas. Africa is a continent which has fifty-three (53) countries and was most likely named after a Phoenician prefix *(Afar)* and Latin suffix *(ica)*, speaking the English language, and classifying their national and racial identity after the name of the land an Italian named after the Biblical Virgin Mary who was an Israelite woman of color.

**Antigua:** "Santa Maria de la Antigua".

**Saints:** The Children of Israel (descendant of slaves) are the LORD's exclusive Saints (Psalm 148:14).

**Who's Your Father?** Who named Israelite's Antiguans?

**In regards to your national identity, Antiguan is a Byword:** Ridicule

**Byword guides us back to our nation:**

    Biblical nation of Israel
    Race: Semitic
    Color of skin: Seven shades of brown
    Language: Hebrew
    Motherland: Jerusalem, Israel

### AFRO-CARIBBEANS

**Historical Highlight**: The Israelite Biblical holocaust of slavery is at the root of American, South American, Caribbean, and global community's social, moral, economic, emotional, and spiritual problems. There will be no peace until the Israelites *(descendant of Negro slaves)* are liberated, justice is executed for the crimes of slavery, and the original Israelites reclaim their homeland ***"Israel"*** from the sons of Esau (the Edomites geopolitical Israelis versus Biblical Israelites).

# BYWORD

**Genesis** 15:13-14 (KJV) "And he said unto Abram, Know of a surety that thy seed shall be a stranger in a land that is not theirs, and shall serve them; and they shall afflict them **four hundred years**; And also that **NATION**, whom they shall serve, will I **JUDGE**: *and afterward shall they come out with great substance.*"

**Origin of the name**: The Spanish called the natives "Caribes" (Caribs) which means cannibals from which "Caribbean" is derived.

**Geography**: Caribbean.

**Demographics**: Israelites remnant scattered in the Caribbean's *(the descendant of slaves)*

*Clarifying the blur national, racial, and color lines*: *The so-called Afro-Caribbeans were transported in slave ships from West Africa to the Americas. Africa is a continent which has fifty-three (53) countries and was most likely named after a Phoenician prefix and Latin suffix, speaking various European languages, and classifying their national and racial identity after the racial reclassification of Kalipunas by the Spanish.*

**Caribbean:** Caribes is Spanish for cannibals.

**Who's your Father?** Who named Israelite's Afro-Caribbean's?

**In regards to your national identity, Afro-Caribbean is a Byword:** Mockery

**Byword guides us back to our identity:**
    Biblical nation of Israel
    Race: Semitic
    Pigmentation: Seven shades of blackness

# Elder Mark Makabi

Language: Hebrew
Homeland: Jerusalem, Israel

## THE BIBLICAL NATION OF ISRAEL

**Historical Highlight:** Abraham, Isaac, and Jacob are our Hebrew founding fathers of the Biblical nation of Israel whereas Jacob name was changed to Israel. The Israelites history of going into captivity in Canaan, Egypt, Assyria, Babylon, Persia, and back into "Egypt" (the Americas) again with SHIPS has been documented. **DEUTERONOMY 28:68 "*And the* L*ORD* *shall bring thee into EGYPT* *again with* *SHIPS*, *by the way whereof I spake unto thee, Thou shalt see it no more again: and there ye shall be* **sold** *unto your enemies for* **bondmen and bondwomen**, *and no man shall buy you."*

**Name origins of Israel:**

> **GENESIS 32:27-28** "And he said unto him, what is thy name? And he said, Jacob. And he said, **Thy name shall be called no more JACOB**, but **ISRAEL**: for as a **PRINCE** hast thou power with God and with men, and hast prevailed. "Israel" means a prince with the power to be righteous in an unrighteous world. Jacob, Israel, Israelites, House of Israel, the House of Jacob, the children of Israel, Hebrews, and Jews are names that are used interchangeable in the Bible.

**Geography**: Jerusalem, Israel, northeast Africa, western Mediterranean Asia. The illegal occupation of our promise land Israel by the Edomites (so-called Israeli) is problematic for the global community.

# BYWORD

**Demographics**: Over 200 million of the 12 tribes of the Biblical nation of Israel scattered throughout the four corners of the earth.

**The Israelite Holocaust of Slavery**: Was God's Judgment on the Israelites for their wicked deeds and is the reason why they were transported in slave ships from West Africa to the Americas. The Arab sons of Ishmael (Muslims) sold the sons of Israel (so-called Negroes) to the Christians European sons of Japheth and the Edomites sons of Esau (*Jewish impostors*) who financed most of the slave ships.

**Semitic Asiatic Heritage** – The origins of the Israelites heritage is in Mesopotamia (Iraq) where civilization began. *(e.g. Babylon and Nineveh)*.

**Abraham:** A Black, Asiatic, Hebrew man that was born in Mesopotamia; **ACTS 7:2** "Brothers and fathers, listen to me! The God of glory appeared to our father Abraham while he was still in **Mesopotamia**, before he lived in Harran. **"There** are **12 tribes of Israel** *Reuben, Simeon, Levi, Judah, Issachar, Zebulun, Dan, Naphtali, Gad, Asher, Joseph, and Benjamin.* The heritage of the so-called Negros out of Sub-Saharan Africa are Semitic, Black Asiatic, and Hebrew Israelites.

**The Biblical Jew:** Judah is one of the 12 tribes of Israel. The second president in Egypt Gamal Abdel Nasser (1956) agreed with Jesus the Christ (Revelation 2:9) *"You have left Black and returned White you are impostors and shall never see peace"*

**The Biblical 12 tribes of Israel:** All Jews are Israelites; however, all Israelites are not Jews or from the tribe of Judah. For example, *Jesus Christ was an Israelite from the tribe of Judah, a Jew (Matthew 1); however, Paul was an Israelite from the tribe of Ben-*

jamin, a Benjamite *(Romans 11:1)* "ask then: Did God reject his people? By no means! I am an **Israelite** myself, a descendant of Abraham, from the tribe of Benjamin."

## THE INVENTION OF WHITE PEOPLE!

**Historical Highlights:** Since ancient times, historical racial concepts varied across cultures which have been misconstrued for various political, social, moral, spiritual, economical, sexual, physical, and emotional reasons. Defining race seems to be culturally subjective. Nevertheless, a common theme for defining race suggests is *persons related by common lineage*. However, to understand the concept of race, we must understand the nature of creation in the mathematical terms of *division*. **Genesis 1:4** *"And God saw the light, that it was good: and God divided the light from the darkness."* Moreover, the division in creation had a heavenly purpose and role for sustaining life; thus, the concept of race is based on the **division** of humanity.

Everything the *God of Israel* created and divided was good; however, after the fall of Adam, everything that the *God of Israel* divided for good could now be used by mankind for good or evil. Thus, it would be at the *Tower of Babel* where men would use their imaginations for evil and where the concept of race comes into effect *(Genesis 11:1-9)*. The concept of race begins with the division of humanity based on **language** and extends to the division of **land** *(origins of geographical location)* and the division of *families (ethnicity)*. For example, The French and the British are the Caucasian sons of Japheth claiming to be white; they are divided by language, geography, and ethnicity. The origin of racial classification based on color can be traced to two European quacks *Carl Linnaeus (1717-*

# BYWORD

*1778) and Johann F. Blumenbach (1752-1840) they **divided** the human species into five races which they classified by color.*

1. **Caucasian race or white**
2. **Mongolian or yellow**
3. **Malayan or brown**
4. **Negroid or black**
5. **Natives Americans or red**

**Origin of the name white:** white comes from the Sanskrit root "svetu" referring to a color not a people.

**Geography**: The Americas, Australia, Europe, Eurasia, and the Mediterranean.

**Demographics**: An estimate 62.6% of the American population are racially classify as a color (White).

***Clarifying the blur national, racial, and color lines***: *The so-called white Americans traveled in ships to the Americas from Europe, speaking their English, French, Dutch, Danish, German, Gaelic, Slavic, Russian, Spanish, Latin, Yiddish, and Portuguese languages, and classifying their national and racial identity as a color and after an Italian named by a German.*

**The Biblical identity of the Caucasian Europeans**:
Gentiles

> **GENESIS 10: 1-5 (KJV)** Now these are the generations of the sons of Noah, Shem, Ham, and Japheth: and unto them were sons born after the flood. The sons of Japheth; Gomer, and Magog, and Madai, and Javan, and Tubal, and

Meshech, and Tiras. And the sons of Gomer; **Ashkenaz**, and Riphath, and **Togarmah**. And the sons of Javan; Elishah, and Tarshish, Kittim, and Dodanim. By these were the **isles of the Gentiles** divided in their lands; every one after his tongue, after their families, in their nations.

## THE WICKED SPIRIT OF SODOM & GOMORRAH IN AMERICA!

The WNBA and their corporate sponsors supported the homosexual community in the sense of condolence for the alleged slaughtered men and women of a LGBT nightclub in Orlando; homosexuality is and has always been an abomination of the Biblical Israelite Nation. However, when WNBA players decided to support the "Black Lives Matter" movement in protest against the slaying of Israelites Alton Sterling and Philando Castile by the terrorist Gentiles Caucasian police, the WNBA fined their own players; later these fines were rescinded. Nevertheless, a moral, logical man, woman, or child has to note that the WNBA as a representative of American culture and values supports people who engage in immoral and unnatural behavior lives are more valued than God's chosen people, the Biblical Hebrew children of Israel in America. Separation!

### Revelation 18:4 (KJV)

"And I heard another voice from heaven, saying, **Come out of her, my people** (Israelite's), that ye be not partakers of her (America's Babylon) sins, and that ye receive not of her **plagues**."

*Woe unto America!*

## BYWORD

## CHRISTIANS

**Historical Perspective**: Contrary to popular opinions the Bible is not a Christian book; it is an Israelite book of the Covenant the Biblical Nation of Israel has with the Almighty God. The death and resurrection of our ***Israelite Messiah referred to as the Christ by non-Biblical Israelites*** *took place during the Hebrew month of Abib (in the Gregorian calendar between March and April).* The Israelites apostles and disciples began to spread the Gospel of Israel under the Mashiah or Messiah, "the Anointed One"; Khristos or Christos is the Greek word for messiah. Thus, the name of Christ spread throughout the Roman Empire which lead to the reputation that Israelites were followers of the Christ in which the suffix was added to coin them as "Christians" between 41-57 AD.

Antioch was a popular metropolitan city and the third largest city in the Roman Empire. Many Israelites including Paul and Barnabas spent time in Antioch preaching about their Israelite Messiah Christ for over a year (Acts 11:25-30).

The more people continued to hear the Israelites preach about Christ, the more the Israelites were called Christians. Calling the Israelites *"Christians"* was equivalent to calling the Israelites captives Niggers in 1619 at Jamestown, VA, a total misnomer.

In addition, our ***Israelite Messiah Christ*** identified himself with his Israelite kinsman Nathaniel ***(KJV-Bible - St. John 1:47)*** and our Israelite brother Paul proudly proclaimed Jesus was an ***Israelite (Romans 11:1),*** and no Israelite practiced the Roman-Greek philosophy of what became Christianity which was against the teaching of Christ. Examples of how Christianity goes against Jesus include: the *Christmas, a Feast of the Winter Solstice based on the*

*Greco-Roman god Saturn Cronos (pagan god of time) during the time of the dead winter, Easter (worship of Ostara or Eostre, a Germanic fertility goddess), Sun-god worship on Sunday, drinking wine at the altar, praying using the symbol of the cross, praying and worshiping Jesus as God versus God's Messiah, baptizing backwards, and celebrating the new year in January winter, Halloween (Celtic pagan celebration of the harvest and transition of souls under Samhain [pronounced Sow'een], pagan god of death), Thanksgiving (a day that proceeds the genocide lead by the British sons of Japheth against the Iroquois peoples of New England) etc. And never refer to themselves as a Christian in regards to their heritage, culture, religion, ethnicity, nationality, or spirituality according to the Bible.*

**Origin of the name**: The author of the book of Acts documented when the Israelites were first called *"Christians"* it was a pejorative.

**(KJV- Bible) Acts 11:26:** *"And when he had found him, he brought him unto Antioch. And it came to pass, that a whole year they assembled themselves with the church, and taught much people. And the **disciples (Israelite's) were called Christians first in Antioch.**"*

**Timeline**: 41-57 AD

**Roman Emperors:** Claudius Caesar Augustus (10 BC-54 AD) and Nero Claudius Caesar Augustus Germanicus (50-54 AD)

**Geography**: Southeastern Europe and West Asia. Turkey (Turkish) Antakya (Antioch) was a populated city of ancient Anatolia near the Orontes River

**Demographics**: Globally an estimate of 2.1 billion people proclaim to be Christians.

**Christians: The Webster Dictionary** - Followers of Christ. This statement is a lie.

# BYWORD

The followers of Christ were Israelites who were called "Christians" as a pejorative by Gentiles.

Christian is mentioned three times in the KJV Bible (Acts 11:26, 26:28, and I Peter 4).

However, no Israelite practice Christianity. Moreover, Peter used "Christian" symbolically as a pejorative in his epistles to his Israelite's brothers who were being persecuted by the Romans i.e. Niggers by the American Caucasian's.

**Who's your Father?** Who called the Israelites Christians at Antioch?

**In regards to your religious identity:** Christian is a Byword-Mockery

More so the practice of Christianity.

Byword guides us back to our religious identity **Holiness.**: The Covenant of the Ten (10) Commandments. (KJV-Bible Exodus 20:1-17 – Matthew 19:17 and Revelation 14:12)

# CNN NEWS
# WHO IS BLACK IN AMERICA?
## "Critical Thinking"

*BYWORD education provides us with the knowledge we deserve to inspire our self-determination and empower us to make the American brand of racism of non-effect.*

CNN News: Black In America Series
Hosted by: Soledad O'Brien
Date: December 9, 2012

**Who Is Black In America Highlights:** CNN "Who Is Black in America? "is a classic example of how America continues to blurred the lines between color and race and the continuation of the horrific miseducation rooted in the anti-Semitic institution of racism in America.

**CNN Who Is Black in America Introduction:** *Are you Hispanic or mixed?*

**Byword the book educational response**: Hispanic refers to

Spanish history, culture or a person who first language is Spanish. Although, Spanish is my first language; it is not my original Hebrew language but the language of my oppressors. Moreover, the Spanish are Europeans; however I am an Asiatic Hebrew Israelite speaking the Spanish language, which resulted from the enslavement of my people in the Americas.

**CNN Who Is Black in America?** *Your school teacher name is Miss Education*: The young woman who claim that she used to classify her race as a Caribbean-American also expresses that when a person claims their Black it does not necessarily mean that they are African-American.

**Byword the book educational response:** The Caribbean is a Spanish term for "cannibal" which was a derogatory epithet and a racial reclassification of the natives Amerindians of the islands by the Spanish. Moreover America was named after an Italian explorer, *Amerigo Vespucci,* by a German; black is a color. Africa is a content, and you're speaking the English language which is not the original language of the slaves.

**CNN Who Is Black in America?** *Is He an object of ridicule?:* A young man identified as Edwin expressed how individuals often ask him if he's black; which he presumes the individuals are asking him if he's African-American. Edwin expressed that he's Dominican and not African American because he believes they are two separate cultures, yet he failed to comprehend their connection as descendants of Israelite slaves in the Americas.

**Byword the book educational response:** Unfortunately, many Dominicans have a shameful reputation for expressing their self-hatred of their melanin to the extent that many Dominicans with very dark pigmentation classify themselves as white during censuses. If the descendants of slaves demonstrated honor, they would be able to articulate that color does not define race, the island of the Dominican Republican *(aka Hispaniola)* was named after a Spanish man named **Domingo Guzman,** the **Dominican *(i.e. African American)*** is a racial reclassification of the slaves by the Spanish and British during the colonialism, and the so-called Dominicans and African Americans are Israelites and have inherited the same Israelite culture.

**CNN Who Is Black in America?** *One Drop Rules!* Nayo is a young woman that has a so-called white father and so-called black mother; however, she was raised with her white father, does not feel black, and claims to be a victim of colorism. However, Becca's parents are from Egypt; therefore she claims to be an African-American since Egypt is in Africa, and she is an American as far as her citizenship. Becca makes a profound and critical statement ***"I never thought being black was synonymous with your color…",* this statement is a classic example of psychological manipulation.**

**Byword the book educational response - Nayo:** It would be interesting to know how the general public would react if Nayo stated that she was Purple. *Carl Von Linnaeus (1717-1778) and Johann F. Blumenbach (1752-1840)* reclassified race by color Nevertheless, it is the responsibility of the parents and the extended family *(i.e. grandparents, uncles, aunts etc.)* to equip their children with the power of knowledge of self in racist America. Therefore, if Nayo mother would have equipped her daughter with the knowledge of her *Israelite (Biblical) heritage,* this young woman would have been prepared to express her racial confidence by being proud to express her Israelite cultural heritage of Rock music among her so-called white peers in her musical rock band and explaining to the so-called blacks that her beautiful complexion is an expression of one of the seven shades of blackness that their Israelite dominant genes produces.

**Byword the book educational response – Becca:** The young woman whose parents are from Egypt and claims to be African-American has a valid argument based on America's racial classification of African because Egypt is in Africa, and she is an American citizen. However, the African-American racial or national identity classification would also apply to *Ethiopians, Kenyans, Algerians, Nigerians, etc. whose children are born in America; thus, the term African-American blurs the blurred lines between Americans of so-called African slaves descent (Biblical Israelites) and African immigrants of children of immigrants directly from Hamitic peoples who attain American citizenship;* Is Becca role to proliferate psychological manipulation and racial confusion among the descendant of slaves and to undermine the 400-year Israelite holocaust of slavery by including many unworthy nations to receive any social, economic, educational, housing, land, and reparations benefits that should be given to "African-Americans?" (Exclusively to Americans citizens who are the descendant of slaves Israelites).

**Byword the book educational responds:** *"My people are destroyed for lack of knowledge:* Ms. Washington was correct to express that Becca *(Hamite)* is not an Israelite *(so-called African-American)*. However, if Ms. Washington had knowledge of her Israelite heritage, she could have articulated to Becca that her Israelites ancestors entered into West Africa from their homeland in

Israel northeast Africa *(not the so-called Middle East)* between 70 and 135 A.D. and were transported into to the Americas in slave ships. Moreover, the Edomite sons of Esau (Jewish), the Arab sons of Ishmael, and the European-American sons of Japheth played a sinister role to erase the names, language, culture, and religion of the Israelites, racially reclassifying them as *Negroes, Blacks, Niggers, Colored, and African Americans*. That is why she *(Ms. Washington)* is not African-American because Africans, Egyptians, Arabs, Caucasians, Gentiles, Edomite's and so-called White-Americans are not Israelites.

**CNN Who Is Black in America?** *The Curious Case of Youssef.* Youssef was born in Philadelphia, Pennsylvania America; however his father is Guinean and his mother Liberian. Therefore, is Youssef African-American, African, American, or Black?

**Byword the book educational response:** The curious case needs to be clarified with the understanding that the seed of your father determines your racial heritage not the place of your birth. For example, a Chinese born in America is Chinese and a Kenyan born in Germany is Kenyan. Moreover, Guinea and Liberia are the West African areas where the Israelite settled; therefore Youssef is most likely an Israelite remnant of West Africa.

**CNN Who Is Black in America?** *Colorism a product of Willie Lynch*: "Colorism is prejudiced attitudes or prejudiced treatment of people based on the relative lightness or darkness of their skin in comparison to others of the same race" (Colorism Healing Organization). Colorism is one of the horrific effects of the Israelite (Biblical) holocaust of slavery in the Americas.

**Byword the book educational response to colorism:** The term

# BYWORD

**"colorism"** is a peculiar term because America's racism was based on color of the so-called Negroes. However, the term colorism blurs the lines between colorism and racism. Colorism is one of the horrific effects of slavery that caused division between the slaves based on their **seven shades of blackness**' to improve social and economic status in America. Therefore, our *seven shades of blackness'* needs to be express in the context of the social, psychological, physical, and immoral conditions of slavery as express in the "Willie Lynch letter that produces the peculiar term **"colorism."** Moreover, the children of slavery needs to stop including nonfamily *(e.g. Becca)* members in our family matters. Furthermore, educating our children on the issues of colorism need to be taught within the historical context of our **Israelite (Biblical) heritage** for effective healing.

    **The Willie Lynch Method (1712)** *"Take this simple little list of differences and think about them. On top of my list is "AGE," but it's there only because it starts with an "a." The second is* **"COLOR"** *or shade.*

    **CNN Who Is Black in America?** *Hollywood's Avatar Scenario:* Tim Wise is the so-called American white expert on racism and the hero with a mission to save the descendant of slaves from his racist ancestors institution of racism and put racist white folks in their place. Who's qualified to define racism? The Israelites (descendant of Negro slaves).

    **Byword the book educational responds:** Although many of the American Gentile sons Japheth may have sincere intentions to address their racist, wicked, and criminal pass for moral redepemton why would the so-called Negro ever entrust them to tell their story of slavery or to define racism? Moreover, history confirms that the European Gentile sons of Japheth have a natural dispostion to morally corrupt our story. If the American Gentile sons of Japheth is sincere in promoting racial and moral redemption they need to be lead, educated, and trained exlusively by Israelites.

**CNN Who Is Black in America?** The Biblical Israelites *(the descendants of slaves)*.

**CNN What Makes You Black?** The melanin.

**CNN Who Determines If You're Black?** The nature of genetics.

**CNN Who Is Black in America?** *Contrast Analysis:* There were no grade school children featured on the program that were assertive enough to articulate their black and proud Israelite heritage; however, the program featured grade school children expressing their self-hatred for their dark skin in the classroom and to her mother. **Classic example of psychological lynching.** Will CNN produce **"Who Is White, Green Purple, or Blue in America?"**

**CNN Who Is Black in America?** *Red Flag:* Is there a sinister agenda? Is this program planting seeds to re-classify the race of the descendant of slaves again or promoting individuals to self-define their race (i.e. sexuality) that is contrary to their genetic, cultural, and ethnic heritage? Was this program produced to continue to blur the lines between color and race of the descendants of slaves to confuse and hide their Biblical Israelite heritage?

**CNN Who Is Black in America?** *Red Flag:* Perry "Vision" Divirgillo, Coach for the Philadelphia Youth Poetry Movement (PYPM) displayed identity signs on a wall. One identity sign was "Gay." Why would the term "Gay" be deliberaly shown on a program about racial identity? Who redefine the term gay? Sexuality is not a culture in itself and is therefore irrelevant to the subject matter addressed in the CNN program. What does engaging in immoral, abominable, and wicked behavior have to do with being Black in America? Is this clip a subliminal message and sinister agenda by the iniquitous LGBT to include and/or to trivialize our Israelite (Biblical) holocaust of slavery as if it is synonymous with the wickedness of homosexuals?

**THE LGBT IS A WHITE-SUPREMACIST ORGANIZATION (i.e. KKK, NAZI etc.)**, spearhead by Jewish (Edomite's) influence. Homosexuals place strife upon themselves based on self-definition according to their mental and sexual dysfunction alone. There is no comparison between the struggles of being "Black in America" with immoral behavior (e.g. rapist, murder, pedophile, theft etc.). One is a blessing of culture, race, and wisdom rooted in our Israelite (Biblical) history and community. One is a choice to turn from the timeless course of nature and away from nature's natural order (**LGBT- L**etting **G**o of **B**iblical **T**ruth). This clip is an excellent example of the European sons of Japheth natural disposition of corruption and why the children of slavery must separate, control, own, and exclusively tell their Israelite story of slavery in the Americas without compromise.

**Psychological Manipulation:** Africa is the name of the continent. Is Becca an Egyptian? However, in my opinion Becca identity is Arab (Arabs currently occupied Egypt), whereas the Arabs are not the Egyptians of antiquity. Thus, why did Becca state she's from Egypt claiming to be an African-American when most likely she's an Arab?

**Becca (Is she an Arab?) "I never thought being black was synonymous with your color."** This statement is blurring the blur lines between black as a color and classifying the color black as a race. Because black is a color which do not determine race. Black is synonymous with color however not race. **A classic example of psychological manipulation.**

**Becca (Is she an Arab?) "Because I thought that was racist who wants to be racist in our society everyone does apparently"** *What's racist? Proclaiming that black is a color or that the color black does not determine race?* Is this statement an attempt to redefine racism? Moreover, *racism* or *Anti-Semitic racism* should be a term that is preserve and exclusively define and apply in the context of the Israelite holocaust of slavery in the Americas.

**Becca (Is she an Arab?) "Because I'm not dark, I'm not black"** This statement is blurring the lines between the color black and colorism, and the beliefs that the color of pigmentation alone determines race. Was the casting of the Becca orchestrated to continue to add layers on the issue of race and to blur the blur lines between color, race, nationality, colorism, and ethnicity to continue to create racial confusion among the Israelites *(descendants of the so-called Negro slaves)*?

### eRace

*eRace slavery, remember the captivity,*
eRace Lynch, remember Willie,
eRace white supremacy remember racism,
eRace the black codes, remember Jim Crow,
eRace white people remember leprosy,
eRace the Negro, remember black,
eRace the color, remember the melanin,
eRace Zong 142, remember the middle passage,

# BYWORD

***eRace the American Dream, remember the Promise Land,***
*eRace the dream, remember the nightmare,*
*eRace Civil Rights, remember April 4, 1968,*
*eRace the 4<sup>th,</sup> remember Attucks' acts,*
*eRace the pledge of allegiances, remember Francis Bellamy,*
*eRace Jackie, remember the Negro Baseball League,*
*eRace the miss, remember the education,*
***eRace Elvis, remember Rock n' Roll,***
*eRace the Negro spirituals, remember the Blues,*
*eRace Master Juba Lane, remember his tap,*
*eRace Teet Tot Payne, remember his country,*
*eRace Public Enemy, remember Hip-Hop,*
*eRace Hip-Hop, remember Tupac,*
***eRace the nigger, remember Acts 13:1,***
*eRace the KKK, remember the Terrorism,*
*eRace the Confederate Flag, remember the Civil War,*
*eRace Birth of a Nation, remember the script,*
*eRace the Birth of a Nation, remember the Birth of a Nation,*
*eRace the stakes, remember the burnings,*
*eRace Emmett Till, remember the whistle,*
*eRace Rosewood, remember Black Wall Street,*
***eRace the slave auctions, remember the sale,***
*eRace the floggings, remember the scars,*
*eRace one drop, remember the rules,*
*eRace Walker, remember the appeal,*
*eRace Harriett, remember the Underground,*
*eRace Tuskegee experiment, remember Plan Parenthood,*
*eRace the Scottsboro's, remember the trial,*

### Elder Mark Makabi

***eRace the blur, remember the lines,***
*eRace Jesus, remember Cesare Borgia,*
*eRace the cross, remember the crucifixion,*
*eRace Zionist, remember Zion,*
*eRace Jewish, remember the Jews,*
*eRace Judaism, remember Judah,*
*eRace Israeli, remember Israelite.*

www.ingramcontent.com/pod-product-compliance
Lightning Source LLC
Chambersburg PA
CBHW061757110426
42742CB00012BB/1891